Also by Logan Clendening, M.D.

THE HUMAN BODY

THE CARE AND FEEDING OF ADULTS

BEHIND THE DOCTOR

These are Borzoi Books, published by Alfred A. Knopf

A HANDBOOK TO

PICKWICK PAPERS

A HANDBOOK TO

PICKWICK PAPERS

LOGAN CLENDENING

NEW YORK · ALFRED · A · KNOPF · LONDON

1936

DEDICATED

to the memory of Lieutenant-Colonel Frank B. Drage, the companion of so many of my English journeys. He knew, I think, every stone and blade of grass in all England; certainly the record of every racehorse, chef, maître d'hôtel, regiment, officer, and second son for the last two hundred years. In whatever spot of eternity Frank landed, it will be for ever England, preferably Old Bond Street at noon in May. And I am sure his first question to St. Peter was: " See here, my good man, which way is the ghost of the Guards' Club? " To which Frank's St.

Peter would reply: " Second right,
first left, sir."

CONTENTS

ILLUSTRATIONS

A HANDBOOK TO

PICKWICK PAPERS

PICKWICKIAN ENGLAND

THE CENTENARY OF
PICKWICK

One hundred years ago, in March 1836, a thin green paper-covered pamphlet called *No. 1 of The Posthumous Papers of the Pickwick Club* was offered to a quite indifferent London reading public. Humble and meek in its beginning, acclaimed by no reviews, it and its successors were soon rescued by the good taste of the man in the street and they were read as no books have ever been read before or since. They were read so diligently, in fact, that the critics were somewhat alienated: for while they recognize that this is the ultimate function of a book, the extent to which Dickens is read has always struck the professional litterateur as slightly vulgar.

To the great army of readers, my own generation, at least the stratum to which I belonged, brought heavy reinforcements. We not only read Dickens, we lived him. Across our dinner-tables we flung the speeches of Jingle and Sam Weller, and Micawber, and Mr. F.'s aunt as the current coin of conversation.

We acted him at Sunday-school pantomimes. And when we went away to war, we chose *Pickwick* as the one book to put in our knapsacks and were perfectly content to go without a marshal's baton there.

My own unbroken allegiance to those pages is the only excuse I have for the production of this anniversary memento. If, indeed, any excuse is needed for so slender an effort, because I have intended nothing more than to bring together for the occasion, from the scattered and now generally inaccessible literature, a description of the external features of *Pickwick Papers* — the history of its publication, a part of its century of praise, the sources of the incidents and characters, and the appearance of the places mentioned.

I wonder whether it will be possible to persuade another generation to read *Pickwick*. I doubt it. Those literary appetites which were whetted on *Sanctuary* and *This Brave New World* will hardly be stirred by situations such as the entrance by mistake of an elderly gentleman into an elderly lady's bedroom, or the clumsy attempts of a pseudo-sportsman to handle a gun. To those lofty people who regard the novel as the sacred place where alone life can be depicted truly and completely, it must be confessed that *Pickwick* is nothing like real life at all, that it has no

" psychology " and that it deals only with the surface and even the superficialities of the surface.

But little as we may be able to analyse its charm, the charm is there. To a large number of people — " unrepentant survivals of another century," as Vincent Starrett says — it remains their deepest literary passion.

My own experience must be that of many of my generation. Dickens was my first classic.

It was my mother who decided I had had enough of Horatio Alger, Jr., and G. A. Henty, and Tudor Jenks (in *St. Nicholas*), Toby Tyler's brother, and Louisa M. Alcott, and *The Story of a Bad Boy* by T. B. Aldrich, and should begin on the real " classics." She was wise in her first selection, for her choice was *Nicholas Nickleby*.

I was sent to the public library to get it — the family was in a period of financial stringency at the time and we possessed in the household no set of Dickens. As I look back on it, our worldly status could be gauged very accurately by whether or not we had a set of Dickens. My father was a kind of semi-responsible Mr. Micawber, if you can imagine such a thing, and at the time I was inducted into the classics we had reached a nadir — so it was the public library. It was a squat one-storey brick building on

Eighth Street between Oak and Locust, in Kansas City. I took out a card and wrote my request, and soon a very dirty copy of *Nicholas Nickleby* was shoved through the window to me.

I was suspicious of it at first. But on the way home I glanced through the pages; there was a picture of Miss Snevellicci in tights and I was apprenticed to the " classics " for ever.

The little boy who sat that summer on the back porch and read *Nicholas Nickleby* was, if any, the gentle reader we all yearn for. When long afterwards I read what Thackeray said: " I know one who when she is happy reads *Nicholas Nickleby*, when she is unhappy reads *Nicholas Nickleby*, when she is tired reads *Nicholas Nickleby*, when she is in bed reads *Nicholas Nickleby*, when she has nothing to do reads *Nicholas Nickleby*, and when she has finished the book reads *Nicholas Nickleby* again," it might have been, save for the gender of the reader, a description of myself. I read and reread *Nicholas Nickleby* for years. The description of Miss Snevellicci in tights was even more provocative than the picture. I wanted to marry Miss Snevellicci and she was only a steel engraving. I thrilled, too, at Gride and the preparations for the secret wedding. Mr. Curdle and his insistence on the preservation of " the unities " both charmed and puzzled me. " Have the unities been

preserved? " — I rolled the phrase for years. But I couldn't find out what they were. Neither my mother nor my father knew. Finally my Uncle Johnny, the Harold Skimpole of our ménage, who was considered to be a patron of the drama, owing to his habit of borrowing enough money from father to go to the Gillis Burlesque Show every Monday night, ventured the suggestion that Pluto had something to do with them. It was not until twenty years later when I was presented to the *Poetics* of Aristotle that I found the answer. My Uncle Johnny never could get Pluto, Plato and Aristotle straightened out.

Not long ago I heard the owner of one of the magnificent collection items of Dickens, for which he had paid a rajah's ransom, remark casually that he should get an abridged " children's edition of Dickens " for his grandchildren. The statement made my blood run cold. An abridgement! What a monstrosity! Give it all to them. There is not nearly enough of the great books — and I will trust a child to reject the bad ones — *Little Dorrit* and *Dombey and Son* and *Great Expectations* and *Our Mutual Friend* and *The Mystery of Edwin Drood* — those written when his brain was hard and his hand was tired.

I went on to *Oliver Twist* and *David Copperfield* and *The Old Curiosity Shop* and even *Bleak House* and *Martin Chuzzlewit* before I tackled *Pickwick*

Papers. It is a young man's book, not a youth's, and I am glad I waited until I was of a proper age.

How long ago that first reading was it would be impossible for me to say — but I cannot remember a time when the sayings of Sam Weller, of Jingle, and of Bob Sawyer were not as much a part of me as my hand or my nose or my eyes. They have been even more satisfactory than those anatomical components because they have not become aged and stale.

When I first went to England, in 1911, all my appreciation of it became suddenly vitalized. Here was the frame from which that glorious picture of adventures had been plucked.

I walked the streets of London, with its strange customs and unfamiliar speech, and despite those embarrassments felt that I had come to the city of my heart. There Macaulay had lived at the Albany, there housing the Wallace Collection was Gaunt House, the town residence of the Marquis of Steyne, out yonder was the garden where Keats heard the nightingale, and round the corner was something much better than prosperity — Baker Street and the lodgings of Sherlock Holmes.

It was all changed from the days of *Pickwick*, but it still was like. And since then *Pickwick* has never left me. I know not why nor how its freshness can

remain and return with each repetition. I only know
that when I am ill, with a cold coming on, or my toe
begins to throb and I take to my bed, the literature I
should catch up on palls, and I open *Pickwick* and
am soothed and delighted. When I go on a journey
I put *War and Peace* or *Crime and Punishment* in my
bag, vowing I will get through this time. There was
an era in Anglo-American criticism, the early Arnold
Bennett–William Lyon Phelps period, which created
an inferiority complex in me that I shall never get
over. Because in this era it was fashionable to say
that the only good novels in the world were Dostoievsky's and I simply cannot make head nor tail of them.
But I keep guiltily returning to them, and, as I say,
in order to ensure that I will get through *The Brothers Karamazov* this time, when I go on a journey I
put it in my bag, and nothing else; then, at the last
minute, I relapse and stick in *Pickwick* and so the
Russians never get read. I am too old to regret now;
after all, what is Holy Russia to me? I still have
Pickwick.

If a book be a great book, to know it should be a
liberal education. And that, even if in the opinion of
some I am not liberally educated, *Pickwick* has been
to me. I do not at all mean that *Pickwick* could ever
furnish a way of life. No one could be so absurd as to

claim that for a book that does not touch at all on tragedy or in which there is nowhere any portrayal of love or hate, or fear, or even ambition.

I do not mean that *Pickwick* has been one of the great formative books of my life. Oh, no; I was emancipated in the orthodox manner by Huxley and Le Conte's *Elements of Geology* and *The Life of Fanny Hill*. Oh, I am sound enough: I know all about the mark of a free man which is an acquaintance, at least in the condensed forms, with the *Areopagitica*, Pareto, and *De Homine* of Descartes.

But *Pickwick* does something else. It gives you courage. It makes you gay. It takes you travelling up and down the great roads of life. It widens your circle of acquaintance. It forms your taste. I still think, after nearly forty years' friendship, it is one of the great books of the world.

Does it show a want of perception on my part — a lack of taste — to be dedicated to a middle-class objective book, skimming the surface of life? If so, I am not alone. The finest minds of our race have paid allegiance over and over again to the qualities of *Pickwick*.

Here is Mr. John Galsworthy's confession:[1]

" Not so long ago I was chloroformed into a public

[1] "Twelve Books — and Why," by John Galsworthy, in *The Saturday Review of Literature*, December 3, 1927 (Vol. IV, No. 19).

declaration of what seemed to me the world's twelve best works of fiction, outside Poetry and Drama. When I came to myself, I began to wonder for what qualities I had chosen that particular twelve; and, for the sake of a clear, or comparatively clear mind, I here set down the result of my wonderings.

" The books were these: Cervantes's ' Don Quixote; ' Tolstoy's ' War and Peace ' and ' Anna Karenina; ' Dickens's ' The Pickwick Papers ' and ' David Copperfield; ' Turgeniev's ' Fathers and Children ' and ' Smoke; ' Dumas's ' The Musketeer ' series and ' The Reine Margot ' series (but only when read in their native French) ; Dostoievsky's ' The Brothers Karamazov; ' Mark Twain's ' Tom Sawyer ' and ' Huckleberry Finn,' and Thackeray's ' Vanity Fair.' . . .

" First, in my cogitation, I perceived that all of these books were very long, with the exception of the two Turgenievs and the Mark Twain. Sheer bulk then seemed to be an advantage, following the maxim of the racecourse — not invariably justified — that ' a good big one will always beat a good little one.'

" I next perceived that all of them without exception were easy to read, putting no strain to speak of on the intellect, either in matter or in style; from this I deduced, either that I was a lazy dog, or that readability was a prime virtue.

"Pursuing my search for common factors, I found that all these books have what I call a 'springy' texture, your mind walks on them as if on resilient turf; it neither skates, as over the polished slippery surface of, say a 'Thais' or an 'Egoist,' nor gets heavy-footed in the valuable clay of a 'Salammbo,' a 'Clarissa Harlowe,' or a 'Père Goriot.' The texture of Cervantes, Dickens, Dumas, Mark Twain, Thackeray, and the Russian Turgeniev, is springier, no doubt, than that of the other two Russians, but even they have a certain resilience of fibre.

"The next and, as I think, very important common factor that I discovered, was that all these books contain one, or more, unforgetable — one might say immortal — characters. Don Quixote and Sancho Panza in the first; Natasha, Pierre, and Prince Andrey in the second; Anna and Stepan Arkadyevitch in the third; Pickwick, Sam Weller, Jingle, and Old Weller in the fourth; Betsy Trotwood and Micawber in the fifth; Bazarov and Pavel Petrovitch in the sixth; Irina in the seventh; D'Artagnan et Cie. in the eighth; Bussy and Chicot in the ninth; the Youngest Karamazov in the tenth; Tom and Huck in the eleventh, and in the twelfth, Becky Sharp. This, indeed, seems a really indispensable feature of the greatest fiction, and the absence of it would rule out any book. Gogol's 'Dead Souls' could not come

in; neither, according to my judgment as to what is unforgetable character, could Melville's ' The White Whale' nor Stendhal's 'La Chartreuse de Parme.'

"When I had got as far as this, I seemed to have reached the end of common elements, unless it were true that all these books had what I call 'familiar spirit.' Proceeding to put them to that test, and discounting for the extravagance of Dickens, the *panache* of Dumas, and the epilepsies of Dostoievsky, I discovered that they do all have that particular quality, and in marked degree. In other words, a reader will live while reading, in the same houses, the same streets and towns and countries, as the people of these books. . . .

"It is indeed something that can be felt about a book but can hardly be described. Flaubert has not got it, except perhaps in 'Un Coeur Simple.' His 'Salammbo' is a marvelous bit of painting, but it remains a picture; and even at 'Madame Bovary,' and her frame, one stands apart and gazes. One doesn't live with her, however one may want to. Hawthorne just misses 'familiar spirit.' Zola never had it; nor Meredith; nor Victor Hugo. Defoe had it in 'Robinson Crusoe' (and in some moods this book would take on my list the place of 'Vanity Fair'). On the other hand, I don't quite feel 'familiar spirit' in Fielding — fine book though 'Tom Jones' un-

doubtedly is. The great Russian writers, one and all, have it in their work; and this is probably what makes Arnold Bennett say that the twelve best novels of the world were all written by Russians. . . . Whether it is the same quality as ' breath of life' I don't quite know, but it is as near as makes little matter. . . .

" In the examination of my reasons for selecting them I started by finding them all eminently readable; I end by considering whether or not they are conspicuously rereadable. I learn from my own experience that they all are; and in the following order : ' The Pickwick Papers;' ' Tom Sawyer' and ' Huckleberry Finn;' ' The Musketeer' series; ' Don Quixote;' ' War and Peace;' ' David Copperfield;' ' Fathers and Children' and ' Smoke;' ' Anna Karenina;' ' The Reine Margot' series; ' Vanity Fair,' and ' The Brothers Karamazov.' . . . To find books rereadable . . . and even very rereadable is, I think, a *sine qua non* of selection. . . . Rereadability can only be judged over a long period of one's life; to stand the test properly, a book ought to be rereadable at almost any age after, say twenty-five, when the sap has finished running up our trunks to all main intents. I think, at the age of sixty, if I could take those twelve books with me to Tristan d'Acunha, where ships only call, it seems, about once in two years, I could get on fairly well for the rest of my

life, without feeling that I was divorced from the world as it was, is, and will be."

That seems to me very sound judgment. There are others. William Morris boasted that if every copy of *Pickwick* was destroyed he could restore it to the world from memory without a word missing. Only the other day so discriminating a critic as Mr. Clifton Fadiman picked out twelve selections in Carl Van Doren's *Anthology of World Prose* as " the most magnificent individual examples of prose," and the trial of " Bardell against Pickwick " is included.

Men of all sorts have risen to acclaim *Pickwick*. Only Sherlock Holmes shares Mr. Pickwick's popularity: only about Pickwick and Sherlock Holmes do people talk as if the characters and places were real. Only the Sherlock Holmes saga else has an examination prepared for it.

Have you ever heard of the *Pickwick* examination paper? It was prepared by that delicate-minded poet C. S. Calverley. I append the account of it written by Walter Besant and published in the Jubilee Edition of *Pickwick*,[1] edited by Charles Dickens the younger:

[1] London and New York: Macmillan and Company; 1886.

THE CALVERLEY PICKWICK
EXAMINATION PAPER.

Some twenty years after the first appearance of
" Pickwick," Mr. C. S. Calverley, a Fellow of Christ's
College, Cambridge, and an accomplished Pickwickian scholar, instituted among some of his friends at
Cambridge a competition for prizes to be awarded
for proficiency in the " Pickwick Papers," and set
an Examination Paper, which, besides displaying
a singular knowledge of the " ins and outs " of the
book, is in itself extremely clever and amusing. By
the courtesy of Messrs. George Bell & Sons, of York
Street, Covent Garden, I am enabled to reprint this
paper from Mr. Calverley's " Fly Leaves; " and I
have also the pleasure of adding a description of
the examination itself, which has been kindly written for me by Mr. Walter Besant, the distinguished
novelist, who was First Prizeman on the occasion.

C. D.

An Examination Paper.
"THE POSTHUMOUS PAPERS OF THE
PICKWICK CLUB."

Cambridge, 1857.

1. Mention any occasions on which it is specified
that the Fat Boy was *not* asleep; and that (1) Mr.
Pickwick and (2) Mr. Weller, senr., ran. Deduce

from expressions used on one occasion Mr. Pickwick's maximum of speed.

2. Translate into coherent English, adding a note wherever a word, a construction, or an allusion, requires it:

"Go on, Jemmy — like black-eyed Susan — all in the Downs" — "Smart chap that cabman — handled his fives well — but if I'd been your friend in the green jemmy — punch his head — pig's whisper — pieman, too."

Elucidate the expression, "the Spanish Traveller," and the "narcotic bedstead."

3. Who were Mr. Staple, Goodwin, Mr. Brooks, Villam, Mrs. Bunkin, "old Nobs," "cast-iron head," "young Bantam"?

4. What operation was performed on Tom Smart's chair? Who little thinks that in which pocket, of what garment, in where, he has left what, entreating him to return to whom, with how many what, and all how big?

5. Give, approximately, the height of Mr. Dubbley; and, accurately, the Christian names of Mr. Grummer, Mrs. Raddle, and the Fat Boy; also the surname of the Zephyr.

6. "Mr. Weller's knowledge of London was extensive and peculiar." Illustrate this by a reference to the facts.

7. Describe the Rebellion which had irritated

Mr. Nupkins on the day of Mr. Pickwick's arrest.

8. Give in full Samuel Weller's first compliment to Mary, and his father's critique upon the same young lady. What church was on the valentine that first attracted Mr. Samuel's eye in the shop?

9. Describe the common Profeel-machine.

10. State the component parts of dog's nose; and simplify the expression " taking a grinder."

11. On finding his principal in the pound, Mr. Weller and the town-beadle varied directly. Show that the latter was ultimately eliminated, and state the number of rounds in the square which is not described.

12. " Any think for air and enterprise; as the wery old donkey observed ven they voke him up from his deathbed to carry ten gen'lm'n to Greenwich in a tax-cart." Illustrate this by stating any remark recorded in the Pickwick Papers to have been made by a (previously) dumb animal, with the circumstances under which he made it.

13. What kind of cigars did Mr. Ben Allen chiefly smoke, and where did he knock and take naps alternately, under the impression that it was his home?

14. What was the ordinary occupation of Mr. Sawyer's boy? Whence did Mr. Allen derive the idea that there was a special destiny between Mr. S. and Arabella?

15. Describe Weller's Method of " gently indi-

cating his presence " to the young lady in the garden;
and the Form of Salutation usual among the coach-
men of the period.

16. State any incidents you know in the career of
Tom Martin, butcher, previous to his incarceration.

17. Give Weller's Theories for the extraction of
Mr. Pickwick from the Fleet. Where was his wife's
will found?

18. How did the old lady make a memorandum,
and of what, at whist? Show that there were at least
three times as many fiddles as harps in Muggleton at
the time of the ball at Manor Farm.

19. What is a red-faced Nixon?

20. Write down the chorus to each verse of Mr.
S. Weller's song, and a sketch of the mottle-faced
man's excursus on it. Is there any ground for con-
jecturing that he (Sam) had more brothers than
one?

21. How many lumps of sugar went into the
Shepherd's liquor as a rule? and is any exception
recorded?

22. What seal was on Mr. Winkle's letter to his
father? What penitential attitude did he assume before Mr. Pickwick?

23. " She's a swelling visibly." When did the same
phenomenon occur again, and what fluid caused the
pressure on the body in the latter case?

24. How did Mr. Weller, senior, define the Funds, and what view did he take of Reduced Consols? in what terms is his elastic force described, when he assaulted Mr. Stiggins at the meeting? Write down the name of the meeting.

25. "Προβατογνώμων : a good judge of cattle; hence, a good judge of character." Note on Æsch. Ag. — Illustrate the theory involved by a remark of the parent Weller.

26. Give some account of the word "fanteeg," and hazard any conjecture explanatory of the expression, "My Prooshan Blue," applied by Mr. Samuel to Mr. Tony Weller.

27. In developing to P. M. his views of a proposition, what assumption did Mr. Pickwick feel justified in making?

28. Deduce from a remark of Mr. Weller, junior, the price per mile of cabs at the period.

29. What do you know of the hotel next the Bull at Rochester?

30. Who, besides Mr. Pickwick, is recorded to have worn gaiters?

THE EXAMINATION.

At the time when this examination was held, the examiner, afterwards so well known by his initials, "C. S. C.," was a young don of Christ's College, Cam-

bridge, still a Bachelor of Arts, and recently elected to a Fellowship. Calverley had at this time a great reputation in the University for cleverness. There are, of course, always plenty of clever men among undergraduates — men who are believed by their contemporaries to be capable of such wonderful achievements as shall reduce the memory of all preceding statesmen, orators, and poets to very insignificant proportions — but there are a few men indeed who have already done wonderful things. Mr. Calverley's verses, which have since placed him in the first rank as a writer of *vers de société*, were already handed about among his friends, though none of them had been published, and the stories of his scholarship, wit, repartee, and readiness were innumerable, though very often of the kind which naturally grows round every reputation. But, as happens with the true humorist, there was in all his work, however trifling, always something earnest, something human. The Pickwick examination, for instance, was not altogether a burlesque of a College examination: it was a very real and searching examination in a book which, brimful as it is of merriment, mirth, and wit, is just as intensely human as a book can be. The characters are not puppets in a farce, stuck up only to be knocked down: they are men and women; page after page they show their true characters and reveal them-

selves; they are consistent; even when they are most absurd they are most real; we learn to love them. It was this humanity in the book which made Calverley fond of reading it and quoting it, and ready to like any one who loved it. The examination — whose exact date I forget, but it was somewhere in the year 1858 or 1859 — was held in Calverley's rooms at seven in the evening. In those days the College Hall was at four in the afternoon, an ungodly time for dinner, but the excuse for choosing this time was that it allowed work to be done in the evening by the reading men. The number of candidates for the prize was, I believe, about a dozen, but the stiffness of the paper and the unexpected ingenuity of the questions made short work of most, and I am proud to say that I had from the beginning but one serious competitor, the present Professor at Cambridge of Anglo-Saxon, Skeat. He was, indeed, formidable, being a man of remarkable memory, wide reading, and a profound student of his Dickens. It was a two hours' paper, and in the intervals of my own writing, as I looked round the table I was disgusted to find that although the other men were mostly gazing into each other's faces with an expression that showed themselves beaten, Skeat, for his part, was doggedly writing on, as if resolved and able to floor the paper. Now, for my own part, I found that I could by no means floor

the paper. The examiner, meantime, clothed in his cap, hood, and gown, marched up and down the room, giving to the ceremony all the solemnity of the Senate House, save for the briar-root which graced his lips.

Before eight o'clock the other men were either sitting back in their chairs, hopelessly, or racking their memories over some obscure point, such as the number of Sam Weller's near relations, or struggling feebly with a question; but the contest was virtually over, and the two prizes lay, quite obviously, between Skeat and myself. Before nine o'clock I had answered everything I knew, had read over and corrected my papers, and was ready with them, numbered, signed, and folded, when the examiner came round to collect them. Skeat, I saw with disquiet, continued writing till the last moment allowed, and I fancied, but perhaps this was due to the jealousy of competition, that there was a slight flush of triumph upon his cheeks as he signed his name on the back, and handed over a bundle which seemed bulkier than my own.

The paper itself has been published in one of Calverley's books, and an account of the examination, or rather a notice of it, has been given in Sendall's "Memoirs of Calverley." It will be found, by any one who will take the trouble to analyse it, a very remarkable document. Not only is it, in itself, an extraordinarily clever paper, but it is a really serious test

paper. No one could answer any of it who had not read and re-read " The Pickwick Papers " and acquired, so to speak, a mastery of the subject. No one could do well in the examination who had not gone much further than this, and got to know the book almost by heart.

Further, it was a most wonderful burlesque of the ordinary College and Senate House classical examinations, considering the subject from every possible point of view, even with the side-lights of contemporary imitation. Especially is it rich in the department then dear to Cambridge scholars, the explanation of words, phrases, and idioms. Some of these which we were asked to illustrate were unintelligible even to the learned examiner, who referred them, with a copy of the examination paper, to the author. Among them was the remarkable expression, " My Prooshan Blue." It was a great disappointment to all of us that, although Charles Dickens acknowledged the paper in a delightful letter, he did not explain what was meant by " My Prooshan Blue." Probably it was a phrase which he had heard in a crowd, and had never asked himself what it meant.

It is pleasant to remember that the examination was followed by a Function much more in fashion in those unregenerate days than now — namely, a supper, of which the leading features were oysters and

stout, with milk punch afterwards, songs, tobacco, and conversation till the small hours of the morning. Calverley's rooms generally showed a light till the small hours.

At four o'clock on the following day, when the dinner-bell ceased and the undergraduates were assembled in the Hall, the Fellows, headed by the Senior, came as usual out of the Combination Room, and walked in single file to the high table. Last of all walked the Junior Fellow, Calverley. At the door he stopped to affix a notice on the screen used for official announcements of examinations, prizes, scholarships, lists, etc. This done, with an air of business and importance, he gravely followed the rest, and took his place where the scholar for the day read the long Latin grace.

The paper contained the result of the Pickwick examination. I shall never again feel so great a joy as that which I experienced when some one read it aloud:

PICKWICK EXAMINATION.

First Prize . . . . . Besant.
Second Prize . . . . . Skeat.
C. S. Calverley,
Examiner.

As for the marks, I believe that the full marks were 1,350, and that I obtained 835. I forget what Skeat, the second man, got. Considering the stiffness of the

paper, it was generally allowed that I had done re-markably well. And I think so myself, to this day.

There was, I think, some feeling among the Seniors, and especially in the mind of the Master, at what was considered a burlesque of the College examinations. If examiners are to be held up to ridicule, what is sacred? The examiner had announced this examination on the official screen, and had pinned upon it the result. He had conducted the ceremony exactly in the same way as if it had been a College examination, in academical costume, the men appearing in their gowns. Surely something ought to be done. I believe that, as a matter of fact, the Master did ask Calverley not to do it again, which, of course, was readily promised, because such a thing could only be done once. And I believe it has never been repeated. There would be no fun in doing such a thing again until the memory of the great original was quite forgotten.

WALTER BESANT.

THE HISTORY OF
PICKWICK PAPERS

Beneath the shining surface of a great book, which is all the reader sees, there lie a thousand incidents, adventures, struggles, despairs, belonging to the author.

To Dickens every one of the six hundred and fifty proper names in Pickwick represented a distinct act of creation, even if that act of creation had been nothing more than the appropriate adaptation of a real place or person, street or building, to the demands of his narrative. Every one of the characters represented two people — the character in Pickwick and the real person who sat for the portrait.

Effortless as its composition seems to us, the backstage career of *Pickwick* was unusually chequered.

It passed through a preliminary period of neglect. It is said that only about four hundred copies of the first number were sold. And that is a high estimate: Mr. Arthur Waugh, the present chairman of Chapman and Hall says that fifteen hundred copies of the

first four or five numbers were put out for sale, but the average sale had not exceeded fifty copies per number.

And then there came the sweep of overwhelming success — which is frequently more difficult to bear.

The first advance of money which Dickens received — twenty-nine pounds — defrayed the expenses of his marriage and honeymoon.

Half-way through the publication there came the deepest personal tragedy of Dickens's life — the death of his sister-in-law Mary Hogarth. He interrupted the writing of *Pickwick* for two months. Mr. Alexander Woollcott has a treasured possession — a pocket-knife with Charles Dickens's initials on it; it was a present from Mary Hogarth and to the day of his death it never left his person. He carried it in his waistcoat pocket when he gave his readings, and it was found on him when he died. The most precious *Pickwick* in parts is the one which he dedicated to Mary Hogarth in his own hand (the Elkins copy).

Besides these major personal events there were annoyances and most troublesome was the incident which occurred during the early weeks of publication and which has come to be known as the Seymour controversy.

No study of *Pickwick* is complete without reference to this controversy. This is again confirmatory of the

thesis I have mildly suggested that to know *Pickwick*
is a liberal education — as if to assure you that an
examination of this book will touch every phase of
human existence. What is lovelier than a controversy?

There are those — weaklings of the world, fearful
to face the rigours of analytical competition — who
are given to writing some such phrase as " It is perhaps unfortunate that the controversy ever arose."
Such cant is not in accord with my own feelings.
Literary controversies and historical puzzles — what
would we do without them? Unfortunate that a print-
er's error perhaps put down " W. H." instead of
" H. W." and began the debate as to the identity of
" the onlie begetter of these insuing sonnets "? Unfortunate that the Dark Lady's name and address
were not included in a footnote?

" My mistress' eyes are nothing like the sun." *

* " I refer to Mrs. Byrd Davenant, hostess of Ye
Olde Englische Wine Shoppe, Cross of St. George,
Oxford."

Andrew Lang tells of an old lady in the Highlands
who, facing her imminent dissolution, sighed resign-
edly and said:

" Well, I suppose I shall soon know the real story
of the Gowrie mystery."

And Andrew Lang sagely doubts whether even in
heaven all the details of that bloody interlude will be

revealed. No, what wise man expects or even hopes to know what Lizzie Borden did on that hot morning in Fall River, where Dorothy Arnold went, whence Kaspar Hauser came, who was the Man in the Iron Mask, what happened to the head of Charles I (on his portrait in Somerset House), what the stone of London really was, what song the Sirens sang, or what name Achilles assumed when he hid himself among women? I do not even care to know definitely and for ever the solution of that latest delicate morsel of literary scandal — the origin of those certain nineteenth-century pamphlets, such as the *Sonnets from the Portuguese,* which were proved by the ingenuity of Messrs. John Carter and Graham Pollard to be forgeries. Let Mr. Wise keep his judicious silence as long as he likes, so far as I am concerned. The controversy is a very pretty one as it stands.

The controversy in the history of *Pickwick* has none of the depth or complexity of those dark mysteries. It is really no more than a difference of opinion. Yet tart words have passed on the matter.

For the story of the origin of *Pickwick* we have the best of first-hand evidence — Dickens's own words. In 1847 he acquired the copyright to all the works he had written up to that time, and issued a library edition for which he wrote prefaces. In the Preface to *The Posthumous Papers of the Pickwick Club* (the

preface still stands in practically every edition since then), he wrote:

" I was a young man of three-and-twenty, when the present publishers, attracted by some pieces I was at that time writing in the *Morning Chronicle* newspaper (of which one series had lately been collected and published in two volumes, illustrated by my esteemed friend MR. GEORGE CRUIKSHANK), waited upon me to propose a something that should be published in shilling numbers — then only known to me, or I believe, to anybody else, by a dim recollection of certain interminable novels in that form, which used, some five-and-twenty years ago, to be carried about the country by pedlars, and over some of which I remember to have shed innumerable tears, before I served my apprenticeship to Life.

" When I opened my door in Furnival's Inn to the (managing) partner who represented the firm, I recognised in him the person from whose hands I had bought, two or three years previously and whom I had never seen before or since, my first copy of the Magazine in which my first effusion, dropped stealthily one evening at twilight, with fear and trembling, into a dark letter-box, in a dark office, up a dark court in Fleet Street — appeared in all the glory of print; on which occasion by-the-bye — how well I recollect it! — I walked down to Westminster Hall, and turned

into it for half-an-hour, because my eyes were so dimmed with joy and pride, that they could not bear the street, and were not fit to be seen there. I told my visitor of the coincidence, which we both hailed as a good omen; and so fell to business.

" The idea propounded to me was that the monthly something should be a vehicle for certain plates to be executed by MR. SEYMOUR; and there was a notion, either on the part of that admirable humorous artist, or my visitor (I forget which), that a ' NIMROD CLUB,' the members of which were to go out shooting, fishing, and so forth, and getting themselves into difficulties through their want of dexterity, would be the best means of introducing these. I objected, on consideration, that although born and partly bred in the country I was no great sportsman, except in regard to all kinds of locomotion; that the idea was not novel, and had been already much used; that it would be infinitely better for the plates to arise naturally out of the text; and that I would like to take my own way, with a freer range of English scenes and people, and was afraid I should ultimately do so in any case, whatever course I might prescribe to myself at starting. My views being deferred to, I thought of Mr. Pickwick, and wrote the first number; from the proof sheets of which, MR. SEYMOUR made his drawing of the club *and that happy portrait of its founder, by which*

he is always recognized, and which may be said to have made him a reality. I connected Mr. Pickwick with a club, because of the original suggestion; and I put in Mr. Winkle expressly for the use of MR. SEYMOUR. We started with a number of twenty-four pages instead of thirty-two, and four illustrations in lieu of a couple. MR. SEYMOUR's sudden and lamented death before the second number was published, brought about a quick decision upon a point already in agitation; the number became one of thirty-two pages with two illustrations, and remained so to the end."

In the 1867 edition the following paragraphs were added at this place. They did not appear in the 1847 edition:

" It is with great unwillingness that I notice some intangible and incoherent assertions which have been made, professedly on behalf of MR. SEYMOUR, to the effect that he had some share in the invention of this book, or of anything in it, not faithfully described in the foregoing paragraph. With the moderation that is due equally to my respect for the memory of a brother artist, and to my self-respect, I confine myself to placing on record here the facts:

" That, MR. SEYMOUR never originated or suggested an incident, a phrase, or a word, to be found in this book. That, MR. SEYMOUR died when only twenty-four pages of this book were published, and

when assuredly not forty-eight were written. That, I believe I never saw MR. SEYMOUR's hand-writing in my life. That, I never saw MR. SEYMOUR but once in my life, and that was on the night but one before his death, when he certainly offered no suggestion whatsoever. That, I saw him then in the presence of two persons, both living, perfectly acquainted with all these facts, and whose written testimony to them I possess. Lastly, that MR. EDWARD CHAPMAN (The survivor of the original firm of CHAPMAN and HALL) has set down in writing, for similar preservation, his personal knowledge of the origin and progress of this book, of the monstrosity of the baseless assertions in question, and (tested by details) even of the self-evident impossibility of there being any truth in them. In the exercise of the forbearance on which I have resolved, I do not quote MR. EDWARD CHAPMAN's account of his deceased partner's reception, on a certain occasion, of the pretences in question."

Behind this statement there is evidently some heat. It was occasioned as follows:

Robert Seymour at the time when he made the proposal to Chapman and Hall was thirty-six years old. London born, he was a well-known cartoonist who portrayed English life in the manner familiar to us all, especially in the work of Cruikshank. His favourite subjects were sporting scenes. He was a man of

unstable temper and subject to fits of despondency.

On the eve of the publication of the second number, he committed suicide. He attached a string to a fowling-piece and in the summer-house of his home at Islington shot himself in the head.

Three of his drawings appeared in the second number.

His death naturally placed Dickens and the publishers in a predicament. They cast around hurriedly for an artist. Among those whom they considered was Thackeray. They engaged first R. W. Buss, whose entire claim to any notice at this day is to be found in the three plates he made for the third number, which must be included in any prime *Pickwick* in parts. He was, however, dismissed and for the fourth and subsequent numbers Dickens and his publishers secured Hablot K. Browne, who drew under the pseudonym of " Phiz." He was, of course, as every reader knows, associated with all the great books in the golden years of Dickens. " Phiz's " great quality was that he was " a marvel of pliability " and " amenable to discipline." [1]

The implication is plain that Seymour was not so pliable and amenable. Dickens and Seymour had a conference the night before Seymour shot himself —

---

[1] These expressions are quoted from J. W. T. Ley's *The Dickens Circle*.

between the time of the issue of the first number and the issue of the second. It may be assumed that they discussed the future development of the story. It may even be assumed that they discussed it *as collaborators* and, from internal evidence which I shall discuss later, Seymour may have suggested that more sporting scenes be introduced. This, however, is pure speculation.

There is, indeed, a distinct feeling of relief when " Phiz " comes on the scene. Dickens is absolutely free to direct things as he likes. The sales had lagged until Samuel Weller appeared (in the fourth number).

Then *Pickwick* took the town, and soon the world, by storm. The sales jumped from the ordinary four or five hundred to thousands. I hesitate to deal in exact figures, for the evidence is conflicting.

Pickwick clubs were formed all over the kingdom. Pickwick chintzes figured in linen-drapers' windows, Weller corduroys in breeches-makers, Boz cabs appeared on the streets — Pickwick canes, Pickwick gaiters, Pickwick hats — there is still a Pickwick cigar which had its origin in those days, although I do not know how direct is the succession from that first product to its modern representative. The thing still goes on, and even today it seems to be believed

that popularity is assured if only one will name anything from a brand of coffee to an hotel by the magic
appellation of " Pickwick."

Carlyle's story makes it all graphic: " An Arch-
deacon," he wrote to Forster, " with his own venera-
ble lips, repeated to me the other night, a strange
profane story: of a solemn clergyman who had been
administering ghostly consolation to a sick person;
having finished, satisfactorily as he thought, and got
out of the room, he heard the sick person ejaculate:
' Well, thank God, *Pickwick* will be out in ten days
any way!' "

Also Miss Mitford's evidence: " So you never heard
of the *Pickwick Papers*! Well, they publish a number once a month, and print 25,000. It is fun — London life — but without anything unpleasant; a lady
might read it aloud; and this so graphic, so individual, and so true, that you could courtesy to all the
people as you see them in the streets. *I did think there
had not been a place where English is spoken, to which
Boz had not penetrated.* All the boys and girls talk
his fun — the very boys in the streets; and yet those
who are of the highest taste like it the most. Sir Benjamin Brodie takes it to read in his carriage between
patient and patient; and Lord Denman studies *Pickwick* on the Bench while the jury are deliberating. *Do*

take some means to borrow the ' Pickwick Papers.' It seems like not having heard of Hogarth."

It was quite natural, in the face of all this exclamatory praise, though equally injudicious, for the family of Seymour to claim for him some of the credit. Mrs. Seymour stated that the central idea and the central characters of this acclaimed masterpiece were not of Dickens's invention, but Seymour's. Whether Dickens replied publicly at the time I do not know. The Preface of 1847, written ten years after the event, is his definite answer.

But there was a sequel. In 1854 Mrs. Seymour published a pamphlet reviewing the entire controversy (see Bibliography, page 140). In 1866 Seymour's son repeated the claims and even attempted a suit for recovery of profits. Dickens, always sensitive to criticism, was thoroughly incensed, and answered the claims again in a letter in the *Athenæum* on March 31, 1866. From that letter were lifted the two paragraphs referred to above as being added to the 1867 Preface.

And here a curious discrepancy appears. In quoting Dickens's Preface above, I italicized one passage. That passage did not appear in just that form in the 1867 Preface, which read: " from the proof sheets of which Mr. Seymour made his drawing of the club and his happy portrait of its founder: — the latter

on Mr. Edward Chapman's description of the dress and bearing of a real personage whom he had often seen."

It must be quite evident that the two statements in the two prefaces have not the same connotation. In the 1847 Preface Dickens gives Seymour credit for the inspiration of the physical appearance and dress of Mr. Pickwick. In the 1867 Preface he takes it away and gives it to his publisher.

In the *Athenæum* article Dickens " repudiated *in toto* all help from Seymour as to ' incident, character, name, phrase or word ' except the sporting tastes of Mr. Winkle " (quoted from Samuel W. Lambert).

The reference to Mr. Chapman's contribution (the " description of the dress and bearing of a real personage whom he had often seen ") is explained by Mr. Chapman's statement made in 1849 that he persuaded Mr. Seymour to give up the idea he first had, which was to make Mr. Pickwick a long, thin man. " As this letter is to be historical," he wrote to Forster, " I may as well claim what little belongs to me in the matter, and that is the figure of Pickwick. Seymour's first sketch was of a long, thin man. The present immortal one he made from my description of a friend of mine at Richmond, a fat old beau who would wear, in spite of the ladies' protests, drab tights and black gaiters. His name was John Foster."

The matter stands, then, in Dickens's explanation, that Seymour had an idea for a book concerning a club of sportsmen. Dickens vetoed this idea except that he retained the idea of a club and one sportsman (Mr. Winkle). He got nothing else from Seymour, and Seymour's drawings were made from his text. Mr. Chapman gave the artist the hint for the general outward appearance of Mr. Pickwick.

This explanation has been accepted practically without qualification by all the orthodox biographers and critics. Except in one case, it has never been challenged. That challenge, however, is very pointed. It was made by Dr. Samuel W. Lambert, in a brilliant little book: *When Mr. Pickwick Went Fishing.*[1]

Dr. Lambert became doubtful of the minor part Robert Seymour played in the inspiration for *Pickwick*, after he had examined a book entitled *Maxims and Hints of an Angler, and Miseries of Fishing*, etc., by Richard Rener. The book was published in 1833 (three years antedating *Pickwick*) and was illustrated by Robert Seymour. One of the characters repeatedly represented is an exact forecast of the subsequent Mr. Pickwick.

I refer the reader to Dr. Lambert's book for a full

[1] Samuel W. Lambert: *When Mr. Pickwick Went Fishing;* with eleven illustrations by Robert Seymour. New York: Edmond Byrne Hackett, The Brick Row Book Shop, Inc.; 1924.

account and for the reproduction of these earlier pictures of Mr. Pickwick's prototype.

It is, however, unnecessary to examine them in order to understand Dr. Lambert's point. The internal evidence he adduces is even more striking and can be appreciated by anyone who has a copy of *Pickwick* at hand. First, on the cover of all the original parts of the *Pickwick Papers* is a picture of Mr. Pickwick in a punt. He is fast asleep, but he has evidently been fishing. " The scene is set on the Thames just off the bridge and church at Putney." Above, Mr. Winkle shoots at a sparrow. The sides of the design show numerous sporting implements, including prominent fishing-rods, landing-nets, etc.

In the entire book neither of these incidents — Mr. Pickwick asleep while fishing, Mr. Winkle shooting sparrows — was ever touched upon. Yet they continued to ornament the covers until the end. Is it not a fair inference that Robert Seymour drew them without reference to the text but with the understanding that the incidents they portrayed would find a place? In other words, it was not so plain to all the parties concerned that the plates should grow naturally out of the text. That, as a matter of fact, Seymour had decided to have quite a hand in the direction of the incidents?

Again, in the immortal first picture of the meeting of the club and the representation of its founder, notice the assortment of fishing-tackle in the foreground. It has nothing to do with the meeting of a literary and archæological club, but substantiates the idea that Mr. Pickwick was to be a fisherman. Here is further plain evidence that Seymour intended to have a hand in things; that the pictures did not grow naturally out of the text but were freely elaborated by the artist.

But all this, of course, Dickens specifically denied.

On Dickens's side I conceive to be the letter he wrote to Seymour between the publication of the first and that of the second issues. It turned up in 1889 for auction at Sotheby's in a scrap-book which had belonged to the Seymour family, along with the original drawings for *Pickwick Papers,* executed in pen and ink and shaded in sepia. They were acquired by Mr. Bernard Quaritch for Mr. Augustin Daly, the American theatrical producer.

The letter plainly indicated that Dickens was exercising his prerogative of supervising the drawings. And courteous though Dickens's objection is, it is easy to see that this disagreement might have been the beginning of the bad blood that existed between Dickens and the Seymour family. It was in response to this letter, evidently, that Seymour visited Dickens,

Seymour's drawing of the meeting of the Pickwick Club. Note the forever unexplained creel and fishing-tackle in the foreground.

Robert Seymour's first drawing for the story of the Dying Clown.
It was to this drawing that Dickens took exception.

Seymour's amended drawing of the Dying Clown

DICKENS HOUSE

48 Doughty Street, London, where the middle parts of Pickwick Papers were written.
Now a Dickens memorial and museum

the only time they ever met, " the night but one "
before Seymour's death:

My dear Sir,

I had intended to write you to say how much grati-
fied I feel by the pains you have bestowed on our
mutual friend, Mr. Pickwick, and how much the result of your labours has surpassed my expectations.
I am happy to be able to congratulate you, the publishers, and myself on the success of the undertaking,
which appears to have been most complete.

I have now another reason for troubling you. It is
this. I am extremely anxious about " The Stroller's
Tale," the more especially as many literary friends,
on whose judgment I place great reliance, think it
will create considerable sensation. I have seen your
designs for an etching to accompany it. I think it extremely good, but still is not quite my idea; and as I
feel so very solicitous to have it as complete as possible, I shall feel personally obliged if you will make
another drawing. It will give me great pleasure to see
you, as well as the drawing, when it is completed.
With this view I have asked Chapman and Hall to
take a glass of grog with me on Sunday evening (the
only night I am disengaged), when I hope you will be
able to look in.

The alteration I want I will endeavour to explain.

I think the woman should be younger — the dismal man decidedly should, and he should be less miserable in appearance. To communicate an interest to the plate his whole appearance should express more sympathy and solicitude; and while I represented the sick man as emaciated and dying, I should not make him too repulsive. The furniture of the room you have depicted *admirably*. I have ventured to make these suggestions, feeling assured that you will consider them in the spirit in which I submit them to your judgment. I shall be happy to hear from you that I may expect to see you on Sunday evening.

Dear Sir, very truly Yours,

Charles Dickens.

The explanation of the matter I conceive to be somewhat complicated, but one perfectly natural to anyone familiar with the artistic temperament and the processes of creation. Dickens, like all creative artists, derived his inspiration from thousands of sources, of most of which he was not aware — hints in conversation, bits of reading, flashes in the street and tavern. He took these into the warm recesses of his mind and fused them into something that was unquestionably, no matter what their origin, his alone. And in the course of time he came to consider that

every particle of the process of creation, including the inciting hints, were his own in origin.

This does not mean that Dickens deliberately misrepresented things in the Preface of 1847 or in the *Athenæum* article of 1866. He wrote them, respectively, eleven years and thirty years after the event. It is not surprising that a man who had a universe of creative work to look back upon should fail to remember the exact circumstances of his inspiration when he was unknown and untried.

When Pickwick was suggested, Dickens was almost without reputation. He was an obscure journalist and free-lance contributor to the weekly and monthly magazines. It was probably because of his obscurity that Chapman and Hall selected him to write the text for Seymour's illustrations: because he would be " amenable " and " pliable." Seymour, on the other hand, had an established reputation. He had conducted several successful enterprises of the kind he proposed to Chapman and Hall. He was thirteen years Dickens's senior. Dickens might, indeed, have demurred somewhat from the terms offered him, but is it natural that an obscure and needy author would jeopardize an enterprise of potential income by overthrowing the entire scheme? Nobody concerned could have had any inkling of the colossal success in store

for the book; to Mr. Chapman, to Seymour, and almost certainly to Dickens also, it must have seemed a publishing enterprise which had a safe but moderate profit in store. It was in the light of the great success that Dickens remembered how categorical he was in rejecting the initial scheme.

Internal evidence itself is enough to show that Seymour's part in the matter was not a minor one. The first chapters do portray exactly what Dickens says Seymour proposed — a succession of the misadventures of a pretentious sportsman who is shown up by the real English country sportsman in the person of Mr. Wardle. Not only that, but Winkle remains always Dickens's favourite among the companions of Mr. Pickwick. He gives Winkle all the " fat " parts. Seymour's influence was more lasting than he knew. It is Winkle who arouses Mr. Potts's jealousy, who is shut out into the night at the Royal Crescent, who flees to Bristol, who makes a fool of himself on the ice, who runs away with Arabella, who defies his father. Snodgrass and Tupman nearly disappear from the later chapters. If, as Dickens says, Seymour put Winkle in his mind, he put in something Dickens never got out of it. After Seymour's death, it is true, the sporting incidents give way to scenes with which Dickens was more familiar — the law-courts of London, elections, poetasters, rival editors, inns, coach-

ing, feasts, the great roads of England, and the debtors' prison — but the vestigial Winkle remains in
sporting attire to the end.

Is it any disloyalty to the shade of Charles Dickens
to accept this explanation? Certainly I cannot see it,
and it is little less than justice to poor Robert Seymour's memory to give him the minor credit due him.

But if he be given that credit, he must accept the
attendant corollary. *Pickwick* became a greater book
as soon as his influence was removed. It was only when
the old trite sporting-novel idea, which had been done
before and was to be done again by Jorrocks and
Sponge and Charles Lever, was discarded that the
glory of *Pickwick* began to emerge. Indeed, I feel a
candid appraisal must acknowledge that Seymour's
pictures, much as we owe to them for realizing Mr.
Pickwick's appearance, were decidedly inferior to
the subsequent ones of " Phiz." " The Pugnacious
Cabman " is very stiff compared to the verve of
" Mrs. Leo Hunter's Fancy Dress Déjeuner " or the
court-room scene or " Mr. Bob Sawyer's Mode of
Travelling."

II

The fictional incidents of *Pickwick Papers* occur sup-
posedly between May 12, 1827 and August 8, 1828.
This is on the authority of Mr. Percy Fitzgerald
(*The History of Pickwick*).

The actual writing was begun probably in January 1836. The first announcement by the publishers was made in February 1836. The first advertisement appeared in *The Times* for March 26, 1836, and announced that " On the 31st of March will be published," etc.

Dickens was to be paid fourteen guineas a number, which he described as " emolument too tempting to resist." He drew twenty-nine pounds in advance to defray the expenses of his marriage and honeymoon. When the great success came, Dickens's emolument was increased to twenty-five pounds a number. His publishers gave him two additional bonuses of five hundred and seven hundred and fifty pounds respectively, at the end of the first year and on the completion of the publication. In all, Dickens is said to have received about three thousand pounds instead of the first agreed two hundred and eighty. The publishers, it is estimated, made a profit of fourteen thousand pounds on *Pickwick*.

Dickens's life just then was very full. " The first number [of *Pickwick*] had not yet appeared when his *Sketches by Boz* . . . came forth in two duodecimos with some capital cuts by Cruikshank. . . . The *Sketches* were much more talked about than the first two or three numbers of *Pickwick* " (Forster's *Life*).

On April 2, 1836, Dickens married Catherine Ho-

garth; the honeymoon was spent at the village of Chalk, near Rochester, which was the scene of the early chapters of *Pickwick*.

When *Pickwick* was begun, Dickens was living in Furnival's Inn, in Holborn. The site is now occupied by the Prudential Life Insurance Company building. Across the way is Staple Inn.

No. 10 is the home of Mr. Grewgious in *Edwin Drood*.

On January 6, 1837, his first son was born, and early in March of that year he moved, almost round the corner from Furnival's Inn, to 48 Doughty Street, which is now the Dickens House and head-quarters of the Dickens Society.

Soon after this, as has been mentioned, his wife's sister, Mary Hogarth, who lived with them in Doughty Street, died very suddenly. Dickens's grief was so extreme that the publication of *Pickwick* was interrupted for two months.

The last number was issued in November 1837. The occasion was celebrated by a dinner with Dickens in the chair, Talfourd, to whom *Pickwick* was dedicated, in the vice-chair, and "everybody in hearty good humour with every other body."

III

The identification of the originals of the *Pickwick* characters has evoked a great deal of ingenuity.

The name Pickwick itself came from the proprietor of the White Hart Inn at Bath. On the front of the Grand Pump Room Hotel at Bath today is a bronze tablet which reads:

ON THIS SITE STOOD
THE WHITE HART INN,
DEMOLISHED, 1869.
ELEAZER & MOSES PICKWICK,
PROPRIETORS.

Moses Pickwick also owned the coaches running from London to Bath, and the conversation between Sam Weller and Mr. Pickwick in Chapter XXXV, as they are preparing to mount the coach for Bath, makes it almost a certainty that Dickens appropriated this particular cognomen. In 1835, a year before *Pickwick* was begun, Dickens was in Bath and Bristol, reporting on an election in which Lord John Russell was involved. He stayed at the Bush Inn, Bristol, Mr. Winkle's domicile during his unhappy seclusion in Bristol. Undoubtedly, the election scenes suggested the groundwork for the election at Eatanswill, so much so that some have supposed that Exeter was the scene intended, although the text plainly says the

Pickwickians took the Norwich coach (Chapter XIII).

Fitzgerald writes that when the name occurred to him Dickens rushed off in triumph to the publishers, calling out: " I have got it — Pickwick."

A descendant of the Pickwicks, we are told, was so bothered after the book appeared that he changed his name to Sainsbury, a far meeker manner of dealing with authors than that employed today by any person whose name some luckless scrivener happens to light upon. The reflection of the modern course of action may be inferred from the announcement in the front of so many current novels to the effect that all the characters and names in the book are fictitious and have no reference to any living person.

As late as the early nineties, however, the name was still extant, as may be seen from the following charming story, taken also from Fitzgerald:

" Two or three years ago a curious and amusing coincidence brought the author's son, a barrister in good practice, into connection with his father's famous book. It occurred at a trial on the circuit.

" Mr. Dickens, who was counsel for the defence, announced that he meant to call Mr. Pickwick. The judge entered into the humour of the thing. ' Pickwick,' he said, ' is a very appropriate character to be called by Dickens ' (*laughter*). With much pleasant-

ness the advocate replied: ' I fully believe that the sole reason why I was instructed in this case *was* that I might call Mr. Pickwick ' (*laughter*), ' and it may interest your lordship to learn that the witness is a descendant, — a grandnephew, I believe, of Mr. Moses Pickwick who kept a coach at Bath, and that I have every reason to believe that it was from this Moses Pickwick that the name of the immortal Pickwick was taken. I daresay your lordship will remember that that very eccentric and faithful follower of Mr. Pickwick — Sam Weller — seeing his name outside of the coach, was indignant because he thought it was a personal reflection upon his employer.' This little bit of comedy harmonizes well with our old Pickwickian associations."

The original of Sam Weller can hardly be ascribed to any one individual. Many Pickwickians who had a favourite " boots " somewhere in the United Kingdom used to write in to claim the honour, irrespective of whether Dickens had ever seen the boots or not.

Sam Weller's speech, so far as it follows the habit of saying " as the so-and-so said when so-and-so," is ascribed to Sam Vale, a popular actor who played Simon Splatterdash, a servant, in a farce called *The Boarding House*. The lines frequently ran like this:

" ' Let every one take care of themselves,' as the jackass said when he danced among the chickens."

" ' I am down upon you,' as the extinguisher said to the rushlight."

" ' Come on,' as the man said to the tight boot."

" ' Where shall we fly? ' as the bullet said to the trigger."

" ' Sharp work for the eyes,' as the devil said when a broad-wheeled waggon went over his nose."

" ' Why, here we are all mustered,' as the roast beef said to the welsh rabbit."

" ' Nibbled to death with ducks,' as the worm said to the fisherman."

Sam's most famous line has been corrupted into " Life is not all beer and skittles." I would wager that few people who use it could tell even vaguely offhand what it means. Sam used it in reference to the prisoners at the Fleet. " It's a regular holiday to them," he said, " all porter and skittles." Skittles was one of the games (ninepins, practically) played in the yard of the Fleet. To Calverley himself is ascribed the first use of the actual words " beer and skittles " in the poem *Contentment*.

Weller senior was immediately recognized by householders on the road from London to Rochester as " Old Chumley," naturally a stage-coach driver.

Mrs. Leo Hunter was suggested — all this, remember, is conjecture — by an enormously rich lion-hunting lady of Portland Place.

Sergeant Buzfuz was Sergeant Bompas, Q.C. Fitz-gerald printed the following letter he had received from his son:

" I am the youngest son of Sergeant Bompas, and have never heard it doubted that the name Sergeant Buzfuz was taken from my father, who was at the time considered a most successful advocate. I think that he may have been chosen for the successful advo-cate because my father was so successful, but I have never been able to ascertain that there was any other special resemblance. I do not remember my father myself; he died when I was eight years old, but I am told I am like him in face. He was tall (5 feet 10 ins.) and a large man, very popular and very excitable in his cases, so that I am told that counsel against him used to urge him, out of friendship, not to get so ex-cited. A connection of mine who knew him well, went over to hear Charles Dickens, sen., read the trial scene, to see if he at all imitated him in voice or man-ner, but told me that he did not do so at all. I think, therefore, having chosen his name as a writer might now that of Sir C. Russell, he then drew a general type of barrister, as he thought it might be satirized. If I can give you any other information, I will gladly do so. My father, like myself, was on the Western Curcuit, and leader of it at the time of his death. I had a curious coincidence happen to me once. A client

wrote to apply to the court to excuse a juror on the ground that he was a chemist, and had no assistant who understood the drugs. It was not till I made the application, and the court began to laugh, that I remembered the Pickwick trial. I believe the application was quite *bona fide*, and not at all in imitation of it.

> " *Yours faithfully,*
> " *John Bompas.*"

The Judge, Mr. Justice Stareleigh was modelled on Mr. Justice Gazelee. He was very crotchety and excitable on the bench. He was the kind of judge about whom the story might be told that he carried his methods of cross-examination of witnesses to his own dinner-table, where once he had a young counsel to dinner and asked him if he would have venison. The counsel replied he thought he would take some boiled chicken, to which the judge replied: " That is not an answer to my question, sir."

Mr. Justice Gazelee resigned in 1837, the year in which the " Trial " appeared.

The Fat Boy was the son of James Budden, who kept the Red Lion Inn at Chatham.

Dr. Slammer of the 97th has been the subject of considerable research. There was a Dr. Sam Piper who was a character at Chatham in 1836. He was peppery and blasphemous, and when *Pickwick* was published seems to have recognized himself to the ex-

tent that he considered calling out the author, and on second thoughts prosecuting him for libel.

A specimen of his peppery style has been preserved in a letter:

New Hill: March 17, '58.

You, the two undermentioned officers, are hereby required to attend at my house, to-morrow, Thursday, at six o'clock, to meet only Dr. and Mrs. ———, also to masticate and wash down your food with good and wholesome wine. In neglect of, or disobeying this order, you are liable to be sworn at.

Gentlemen, yours sincerely,
Sam Piper.

Mr. van Noorden, however, is not satisfied with this identification, as can be seen from the following paragraph in his introduction to the Topical Edition:

" The reiteration of the title of the 97th Regiment to which Dr. Slammer belonged attracted my attention, and on searching in old Army Lists I find that Matthew Lamert, the army surgeon and prototype of Slammer, a relative of Dickens by marriage, did not belong to that regiment. Yet one Joseph Richard Lamert was an ensign of the 97th from 1825–1832, and was doubtless another relation. We possibly have his portrait in the Hon. Wilmot Snipe. Matthew Lamert (Dr. Slammer) received his commission in

1801, and was surgeon of the 1st Royal Veteran Battalion in 1821. The regiment was disbanded in 1826, when he was placed on half pay. He entered the 91st Regiment of Foot in 1827, and retired on half pay, July, 1830."

Jingle is associated with Charles Matthews, the elder, who used to tell tall tales in a staccato fashion, one being of a lady in India whose husband, when she was burned to death, called in the native servants to " sweep her up."

Tracy Tupman was modelled upon a Mr. Winter, a stout buck who was very susceptible and elegant in his attentions to the ladies.

IV

The illustrators of Pickwick comprise a subject of their own. Besides the original three — Seymour, Buss, and Browne — Leech and Thackeray were both considered as successors to Seymour. Leech's sketch (he was only eighteen) of Tom Smart and the chair has been preserved and it is a beauty.

Then there were William Heath (1837), " Alfred Crowquill " (1837), Thomas Onwhyn (1837), F. W. Parlthorpe (1847), Thomas Sibson (1838), Kenny Meadows (1838), C. R. Leslie (1847), Sir John Gilbert (1847), J. Grego (1861), Christopher Coveny (1883), J. C. Clark (" Kyd ") (1890), Frank

Reynolds (1910), Cecil Alden (1910), and John Austen (1933). American illustrators include F. O. C. Dailey (1888), S. Eytinge, Jr. (1867), Thomas Nast (1873), A. B. Frost (1881).

It can hardly be said that any of them are successful. The modern ones are ghastly failures. The early ones suffer from a look of unreality. It is common to so many illustrations of Victorian novels — Thackeray's for his own books, and Cruikshank's. The artists have piled Ossa on Pelion and added satire to the caricatures of Dickens.

Seymour's sepia sketches would have been great improvements on the ones that were published. " Phiz " redrew for the Household Edition of 1874 an entire new set of plates, which are my favourites, perhaps because they were in the first edition I ever read.

But there are certain characters they all miss. They do well enough with Mr. Pickwick, and Winkle, and Tupman, and Snodgrass, and Old Mr. Weller, but they all muff Sam Weller. Perhaps he was too much for them. It has always seemed to me that Sam must have been rather handsome: he was quite a hand with the ladies, and the pretty housemaid could hardly have been captivated by the rakish and wizened smart Aleck that always stands for Sam. The only Sam which comes up to my ideal is the portrait of the actor W. J. Hammond, who represented him on the stage.

W. J. Hammond as Sam Weller in the stage piece. Isn't it more likely that Sam Weller appeared like this than as he is usually pictured?

C. R. Leslie's drawing of Mr. Pickwick and Mrs. Bardell, which hung in Dickens's
library in Gad's Hill House

Nor are the ladies ever done justice. Mary has never been made pretty enough to suit me. And surely Mrs. Weller was not the gross female she is depicted. Buxom she might have been, but in a handsome way. F. O. C. Dailey shows her thus. Mrs. Bardell, too, must have been softer, more like the painting of her by C. R. Leslie which hung in Gad's Hill until Dickens's death.

V

Pickwick's imitators and *Pickwick* on the stage are matters that few real Pickwickians can view with complacency or even authority. How would it be possible for anyone who had once quaffed at the source to read Reynolds's *Pickwick Abroad?* The irascible Mr. Pickwick there depicted is not ours nor the world's.

Even before the final monthly parts were issued, several dramatized versions were appearing on the London stage. *The Peregrinations of Pickwick* by William Leman Rede was produced at the Adelphi Theatre on April 10, 1837 (nearly six months before the last issue was on the streets, September 27, 1837).

In order to obtain any dramatic coherence the adapters built the plot around " The Story about a Queer Client," one of the incidental interruptions in *Pickwick,* which no true Pickwickian reads. The ac-

tors and actresses were chosen because of their imme-
diate popularity and, like the infant phenomenon,
they had specialties in the form of songs or dances,
all of which were worked into the proceedings
somehow.

The nature of the performance may be gathered
from the program:

ACT I. — THE MISER FATHER

Old Clutchley (a wealthy speculator)	Mr. O. Smith
George Heyling	Mr. Hemming
Maria (betrothed to Heyling) .	Mrs. Yates
Norah (attendant on Miss Wardle)	Mrs. Fitzwilliam

THE CLUB

Charing Cross — CAB-*alistic Doings — A Meeting — A Journey*

SAMUEL PICKWICK, Esq. (Founder of the P.C., a gentleman of the inquiring sort)	Mr. Yates
Augustus Snodgrass, Esq., M.P.C.	Mr. Stirling
Tracy Tupman, Esq., M.P.C. .	Mr. Ismay
Alfred Jingle (NOT) Esq. (a gentleman of a talkative sort) . .	Mr. Buckstone

THE ELOPEMENT

Garden — A Father's Denunciation — The Flight
Air, "*O! Killarney's Lucid Lake*"
  (Old Irish Melody) . . . Mrs. Fitzwilliam

THE BALL AT ROCHESTER

Ante-room at Ball. — Arrival of Visitors. — Pick-
  wickians Pleasuring. — Cutting Out and
    Cutting In. — Fighting and Flirting.

A. Wardle, Esq., of Dingley Dell
  (an old English Gentleman) . Mr. Cullenford
Dr. Slammer, M.D. . . . . Mr. Sanders
Joe ("The Fat Boy" — a peri-
  patetic somnambulist) . . . Mr. Dunn
Miss Wardle (maiden sister of
  Mr. Wardle) . . . . . Mrs. Young
The Misses Wardle . . . . {Miss A. Conway
                       {Mrs. Forsythe

Quadrille. — Another Elopement. — Pursuit.

ACT II. — WHITE HART INN, BOROUGH
Arrival of Pursuers. — The Interview. —
    The Compromise.

Sam Weller (Boots, with original notions respecting things in
  general) . . . . . . Mr. John Reeve

Mr. Perker (an Attorney) . . Mr. Young
Ostler . . . . Mr. Gifford
Chambermaid . . . . . . Miss Conway

THE MARSHALSEA PRISON

*Destitution. — Unforgiving Father. — Generous
Hibernian. — Catastrophe.*

Air, " *The Grave where the Dear
One Died* " (Irish Melody) . Mrs. Fitzwilliam

SPORTSMEN (Country and Cockney)

*The Banquet. — Precautions. — Effects of Punch
and Speech-Making.*

Of course it is not true that Dickens gave permission for these piracies. On the contrary, he writhed and stormed at them. Upon the head of the author of one version he emptied the vials of his wrath. The wretch had been commissioned to write seven melodramas for the " City Company," " to enable him to do which a room had been hired in a gin shop close by." Bacchus triumphed over Melpomene and the dramas were never produced, although from Dickens's words we may assume that the author wheedled some money from the producers — " Well, if it be the means of putting a few shillings in the vermin-

eaten pockets of so miserable a creature, let him empty out his little pot of filth and welcome."

The most successful (and respectable) of the stage productions was the adaptation of W. T. Moncrieff, called *Sam Weller, or The Pickwickians*, a burletta in which Mr. W. J. Hammond played Sam (see illustration, page 58).

Mr. J. Lee was Alfred Jingle, a performance not duplicated until a young man from the provinces named Henry Irving undertook the role in a different version on October 23, 1871.

THE TOPOGRAPHY OF
PICKWICK PAPERS

Even an ardent Pickwickian might read on in the book's flowing pages and never orient himself as to exactly where the Pickwickians went on their travels and in what spots of England their adventures occurred.

As to why they went to these different places, that is a different matter. The glorious thing about the pilgrimage is that they never had any very clear reason for going anywhere. Oh, they pretended to follow Mr. Jingle for a time in order to bring him to justice, but they were caught up in a whirl of other events as soon as they arrived in his vicinity, and most of the time they journeyed as aimlessly as if they had put a pin, blindfolded, in a map.

For one who is leisurely and sentimentally inclined about Dickens, there could be no more amusing and instructive way of spending a summer fortnight in England than in making the Pickwickian pilgrimage and visiting the spots mentioned in the *Papers*. The

journey will take you into parts of England of delightful literary and historical association quite apart from any *Pickwick* or Dickens interest.

My wife and I have taken many of these trips and last summer made the complete round again. And *Pickwick* is remembered — the old inns are there, all keeping the tradition roaring, the streets, the houses, many of them bearing memorial plaques.

We had hoped that our friends Mr. Alexander Woollcott and Mr. Vincent Starrett would accompany us. The scheme had been inspiredly broached one afternoon when we had forgathered at Mr. Woollcott's famous apartment " Wits' End " (where the company is always capable of giving you a sneerful). Mr. Woollcott's addiction to Dickens has been incorporated in many of his eternally delightful writings, and Mr. Starrett, besides being the eminent biographer of Sherlock Holmes, is a Droodian of the deepest dye, whose complete collection of solutions of *The Mystery of Edwin Drood* is to be the basis for a, to me, long awaited definitive Sherlockian analysis of the matter. They were thus eminently qualified to be leaders of a Dickens expedition. But when the time came, larger duties prevented them — mysterious messages from the East indicate to me that someone looking equally like Augustus Snodgrass, Sherlock Holmes, and Mr. Starrett is holding secret confer-

ences under the shadow of the Great Wall of China, and no less mysterious (to me, who have no imaginative conception of ether waves) communications emanating from a plain oak box in my library, with the familiar cadences of Mr. Woollcott, suggest that he has installed a microphone at " Wits' End."

My wife and I made the Pickwick pilgrimage with only the memories of our friends to accompany us. Sometimes we speculated on what might have been, a procedure which greatly puzzled the Colonel, Lieutenant-Colonel Frank Drage, of Chapel Brompton, Northamptonshire, whom we always routed out in England and in whose society we both delighted.

In following the path of the Pickwickians we are directed very specifically by Dickens himself. Except in such instances as Dingley Dell, where the use of the actual name might embarrass the people living there, or Eatanswill, where the events described might be resented if an actual town were named, he does not resort to fictitious titles for cities, inns, or streets. And most of these still remain for the edification of such inveterate and unrepentant sightseers as Mama, the Colonel, and myself.

The Pickwick Club empowered Mr. Samuel Pickwick, Mr. Tracy Tupman, Mr. Augustus Snodgrass, and Mr. Nathaniel Winkle to travel and forward authenticated accounts of their journeys. The club

cordially recognized the principle of every member of the Corresponding Society defraying his own expenses.

For no reason mentioned in the text, they had resolved to go to Rochester first.

Near Rochester is Cobham, and somewhere thereabouts is Mr. Wardle's farm, Dingley Dell.

After a return to London they journeyed into East Anglia somewhere in the neighbourhood of Norwich. On the same trip they visited Bury St. Edmunds.

Again, after returning to London, they went northeast to Ipswich.

After Mr. Pickwick's trial in London, they went, for no better reason than to see the country, into the west to Bath.

One more trip which they took after Mr. Pickwick's release from prison was through the middle northern counties, to Birmingham, and back to London by way of Daventry and Towcester.

If you have followed these points on the map, you will see what a large part of England is comprehended in the Pickwickian pilgrimage.

London is the hub from which all the Pickwickian journeys radiate.

For purposes of description it will be convenient to lump the London adventures together and consider first:

PICKWICKIAN LONDON

Mr. Pickwick's London lodgings were in Goswell Street and he took the famous cab and the famous cab-horse from thence to the Golden Cross. Goswell Street still remains, fallen upon evil days, now called Goswell Road, for devoted Pickwickians to goggle at. It is in the neighbourhood of Islington.

It is not easy for me to visualize the London of Mr. Pickwick's day. Trafalgar Square and the Nelson Column did not exist. Buckingham Palace would have been unrecognizable. It was not used as a royal residence until 1837, when Queen Victoria chose it as her town residence. The Mall had not been parked as an avenue to connect the two landmarks, the Palace and the Square.

The sort of centre of London activity represented today by Trafalgar Square was probably taken up by the Inns of Court, Temple Bar, and their environs. The Thames, however, flowed unrestrained at the foot of the Temple Gardens; the Embankment dates from 1864 to 1870.

The Houses of Parliament as we know them now were not completed until 1857. The corner-stone was laid in 1840. The old houses were burned down in 1834.

The National Gallery was erected 1832–8.

The original Phiz drawing of the White Hart Inn. Note the similarity of the galleries to those at the George.

THE GEORGE, SOUTHWARK

*The last of the old coaching inns. Near by stood the White Hart,
where Sam Weller was boots.*

Mr. Pickwick's London sprawled on both sides of the river. The fashionable residence district for the rich merchant-banker middle class was Bloomsbury, Russell Square, and Bedford Square. The great ducal houses, Marlborough House, Stafford House, Lansdowne House, Grosvenor House, Dorchester House, and Chesterfield House were in a district of parks and gardens. Of them only Chesterfield House and Marlborough House remain, fulfilling their original purposes. Stafford House (afterwards Lancaster House) contains the fascinating London Museum. Grosvenor, Dorchester, and Lansdowne Houses are now hotels.

The City was much the same as at present, I suppose. Temple Bar (the real Temple Bar) was in its place. Regent Street was a colonnaded promenade. Hampstead stretched away to the north as at present. The Haymarket was the theatre district.

The Inn of the Golden Cross, whence the " Commodore," the coach to Rochester, regularly departed, no longer stands, but since it occupied the site where Nelson's monument now rears its — well, rears itself, to be plain about the matter — there will be no difficulty in finding the historical spot — where we intend to be photographed before entering car for Rochester ourselves. (The Golden Cross Hotel indeed does have an existence; fronting Charing Cross Station — but

this is the *new* hotel, a mere parvenu which was erected in 1831–2. I am assured that the Golden Cross to which Dickens referred — the *old* hotel — stood or rested where Nelson's monument rears itself, as above mentioned.)

After the Rochester episodes which make up the first few chapters, the Pickwickians returned, dramatically and in great haste, to London. It was May 23, 1827, according to Percy Fitzgerald. Mr. Jingle had eloped with the maiden aunt, and Mr. Wardle and Mr. Pickwick set out to find them.

" There are in London several old inns, once the headquarters of celebrated coaches in the days when coaches performed their journeys in a graver and more solemn manner than they do in these times," begins Chapter X. " In the Borough especially, there still remain some half dozen old inns, which have preserved their external features unchanged, and which have escaped alike the rage for public improvement, and the encroachments of private speculation. Great, rambling, queer, old places they are, with galleries, and passages, and stair-cases, wide enough and antiquated enough, to furnish materials for a hundred ghost stories, supposing we should ever be reduced to the lamentable necessity of inventing any, and that the world should exist long enough to exhaust the innumerable veracious legends connected with old Lon-

don Bridge, and its adjacent neighbourhood on the Surrey side."

To one of them, the White Hart, we go in imagination, and with Mr. Wardle and Mr. Pickwick and Mr. Perker we have the supreme adventure of meeting Sam Weller.

In imagination only can we go to the White Hart. It had a long career. It is mentioned in the Second Part of Shakspere's *Henry VI* (Act IV, Scene viii). Cade says : " Hath my sword therefore broke through London gates, that you should leave me at the White Hart in Southwark? " But that long career is ended. There is no White Hart in Southwark. The original was destroyed by the fire of 1676 and rebuilt in the form described in *Pickwick*. But in 1889 this inn was demolished. The only relic from it is a baluster from " the old clumsy balustrade "; it reposes in the Dickens House, 48 Doughty Street. But near where it stood is the George Inn, which should be visited by all Pickwickians.

You go over London Bridge and turn into the High Street. With little trouble you should find the entrance to the courtyard of the George. The open balcony might have been the one drawn by " Phiz " in the famous plate of the meeting of Wardle, Pickwick, and Perker with Sam Weller.

The George has traditions, too. Thinking that per-

haps there was some mistake because the George looked so much like the picture of the White Hart, I asked the proprietress if any White Hart Inn was near by. She replied in the negative.

I then suggested, as the English legal cross-examination has it, that perhaps the George used to be called the White Hart.

I struck fire there. With a toss of her head, " There has been a George here for five hundred years," she boomed.

The George well repays a visit on its own account. Nowhere else in England, that I know of, do you find an old coaching inn with a balcony. From the George, Dr. Johnson probably took coach when he visited Mr. Thrale at Streatham. The George itself has appeared in a novel of its own, *The Amateur Gentleman* by Jeffrey Farnal.

You will want to sit in the picturesque coffee-room and remember the " Moor Eeffoc " of *David Copperfield*.

Every year on the Saturday nearest Shakspere's birthday, April 23, a Shakspere pilgrimage, starting from Southwark Cathedral, halts at the site of the Globe Theatre and concludes its celebration in the yard of the George. Scenes from one of Shakspere's plays are acted from a lorry by the Overian Players, a group of workingmen actors.

WHERE THE PICKWICKIANS SET OFF FOR ROCHESTER

Barracks and old houses on the site of Trafalgar Square, 1826 (From Haunted London, by Walter Thornbury, 1865)

LANT STREET, IN THE BOROUGH

Bob Sawyer's lodgings were here.

"Lant Street, Borough: it's near Guy's and hand for me, you know. Little distance after you've passed St. George's church — turns out of the High Street on the right hand side of the way."

"There is a repose about Lant Street in the Borough which sheds a gentle melancholy upon the soul. There are always a good many

*houses to let in the street: it is a bye-street too, and its dulness is
soothing. A house in Lant Street would not come within the denomina-
tion of a first-rate residence, in the strict acceptation of the term;
but it is a most desirable spot nevertheless. If a man wished to ab-
stract himself from the world — to remove himself from within the
reach of temptation — to place himself beyond the possibility of any
inducement to look out of the window — he should by all means go
to Lant Street."*

ROCHESTER CATHEDRAL

Dickens is also remembered and celebrated in the courtyard of the George. In February 1934 the Tabard Players commemorated the one hundred and twenty-second anniversary of Dickens's birth with a performance of a dramatic adaptation of *David Copperfield*.

You are now in the Borough and should visit the Marshalsea Prison, mentioned in " The Old Man's Tale about the Queer Client." " In the Borough High Street, near Saint George's Church, and on the same side of the way, stands, as most people know, the smallest of our debtors' prisons — the Marshalsea."

With some trouble you may also find Lant Street. If you ask an inhabitant of the Borough the way to Lant Street, he is likely to reply mysteriously, accompanied by the usual " three to the right and four to the left," with the cryptic remark: " There is a big kettle there." Not until you see the head of the street do you understand what he means, but the accompanying illustration will make it clear.

" ' There's my lodgings,' said Mr. Bob Sawyer, producing a card, ' Lant Street, Borough; it's near Guy's, and handy for me, you know. Little distance after you've passed Saint George's Church — turns out of the High Street on the right hand side of the way."

Here also you should visit or at least walk past the

entrance of Guy's Hospital, where Mr. Sawyer and Mr. Allen pursued their studies; it is one of the most famous institutions for the treatment of the sick in the world.

The London visitor will find many things of Dickens interest. No true Pickwickian, I am sure, will fail to visit the Dickens House, at 48 Doughty Street. In the basement is a reproduction of the kitchen at Dingley Dell. Here also you may see a Pope Joan board, the game which Mr. Pickwick and the old lady played. The house is crowded with mementoes and has a complete and valuable library.

The secretary and the editor of *The Dickensian,* respectively Mr. Dexter and Mr. Edwards, are most courteous, affable, and painstaking in their reception of visitors. I have a notion that they would quite turn themselves inside out to be nice to a visitor who contemplated presenting them with a *Pickwick* in parts.

A visit to the South Kensington Museum to see the most complete collection of Dickens manuscripts in the world should also be a feature of the London visit.

In Holborn a large red-brick building occupied by the Prudential Insurance Company is on the site of Furnival's Inn, where Dickens had chambers from 1834 to 1837 and where he began to write *Pickwick Papers.* When one or two numbers had been published he removed to 48 Doughty Street, the Dickens House,

and it was there that most of *Pickwick* was written; it was finished at Broadstairs. Mr. Grewgious in *The Mystery of Edwin Drood* found accommodations for Rosa at Furnival's Inn.

Not far down the street is the site of the Black Bull in Holborn, where Mrs. Gamp and Betsey Prig nursed Mr. Lewsome. Across the street from the Prudential Insurance building is Staple Inn, a lovely bit of Old London. It is still much as it must have been when accurately described in *Edwin Drood:*

" Behind the most ancient part of Holborn, London, where certain gabled houses some centuries of age still stand looking on the public way, as if disconsolately looking for the Old Bourne that has long run dry, is a little nook composed of two irregular quadrangles, called Staple Inn. It is one of those nooks, the turning into which, out of the clashing street, imparts to the relieved pedestrian the sensation of having put cotton in his ears, and velvet soles on his boots."

Every sightseer of literary tendencies will enjoy a visit north to Hampstead and Hampstead Heath. So far as *Pickwick* association is concerned, the Hampstead Ponds appear on the very first page, being the subject of a paper communicated by Samuel Pickwick, Esq., G.C.M.P.C., entitled " Speculations on the Source of the Hampstead Ponds, with Some Ob-

servations on the Theory of Tittlebats." The Hampstead Ponds are still in view, a playground now for children, on which they sail their boats unmindful of the profound researches mentioned above.

In Hampstead Lane we pass the Spaniards Inn on the right. It was here that Mrs. Bardell, Mrs. Raddle, and other friends spent the afternoon when they were found by Mr. Jackson, clerk of Dodson and Fogg, and conveyed to the Fleet Prison for costs in the action of Bardell versus Pickwick.

"They all arrived safely in the Spaniard Tea-gardens, where the luckless Mr. Raddle's very first act nearly occasioned his good lady a relapse: it being neither more nor less than to order tea for seven, whereas (as the ladies one and all remarked), what could have been easier than for Tommy to have drank out of anybody's cup, or everybody's, if that was all, when the waiter wasn't looking, which would have saved one head of tea, and the tea just as good!"

Hampstead Heath opens out just beyond the Spaniards.

And here one of the great sights of London, which the average visitor all too frequently misses, is Ken Wood, formerly the residence of Lord Mansfield, mentioned in *Barnaby Rudge*, which the Gordon rioters endeavoured to destroy. By the gift of Lord Iveagh it is the property of the Crown and is open

to the public on week-days from ten to five. It is a typical and beautiful Georgian house, with a library designed by Adam intact, which, so far as interior decoration is concerned, is one of the great sights of the world.

On the way back we should look at Well Walk, where Keats lodged, and then visit the Keats House at Lawn Bank, which is now maintained as a Keats memorial and museum. In the garden there he wrote the *Ode to a Nightingale*.

Not far away is Jack Straw's Castle, where frequently Dickens and Forster forgathered for a red-hot chop and a glass of good wine.

Another Pickwickian landmark is Dulwich, in a different direction from Hampstead Heath. Dulwich was the spot chosen for Mr. Pickwick's residence in retirement. " ' The house I have taken,' said Mr. Pickwick, ' is at Dulwich; it has a large garden, and is situated in one of the most pleasant spots near London.' " A Pickwick Villa is pointed out by the elderly inhabitants of Dulwich.

At Dulwich Church Mr. Snodgrass was married to Emily.

The Dulwich picture gallery is open for inspection. Whether the same one in which Mr. Pickwick could " still be frequently seen, contemplating the pictures," I do not know.

Certain famous London sights visited by all are of Pickwickian interest. The Guildhall, where was the Court of Common Pleas, was the scene of the trial of Bardell versus Pickwick. The Inns of Court, particularly Gray's Inn, were evidently favourites with Dickens. They appear again and again in his novels, and no wonder. They can be reached in a short walk from Doughty Street, and as one muses in the pleasant gardens, one seems to be far away from the busy modern world. The catalpa trees are said to have been planted by Francis Bacon, who was admitted a member of Gray's Inn in 1576 at the age of fifteen. In the great hall the *Comedy of Errors* is believed to have been acted in 1594.

While you are in that neighbourhood, you might wish to visit Russell Square in the Bloomsbury district. In Montague Place, just behind the British Museum, was the home of Mr. Perker, and in Russell Square itself those other families in another cycle, the Sedleys and Osbornes, lived.

But we cannot take time to mention all the London associations of Dickens. For those who wish to pursue the matter further, there is a little book by Walter Dexter called *The London of Dickens,* and with this in hand and following the routes that he advises, you will learn not only a great deal about Dickens, but also a great deal about London.

ROCHESTER

" I have at this moment got Pickwick, and his friends, on the Rochester coach," wrote Dickens to Catherine Hogarth, on March 18, 1836, " and they are going on swimmingly, in company with a very different character from any I have yet described, who I flatter myself will make a decided hit. I want to get them from the Ball, to their Inn, before I go to bed — and I think that will take me until one or two o'clock, *at the earliest*. The Publishers will be here in the morning, so you will readily suppose I have no alternative but to stick at my desk."

Of all the *Pickwick* shrines, the most important is undoubtedly Rochester. And of all the jaunts from London, it is the one that may most profitably be made by automobile.

Leaving London at 11 a.m. we arrive at Rochester, on modern travelling schedules, at 12.30 p.m.

Before we enter Rochester, though, we should take a short turning (this is why the automobile is more convenient for this trip) and visit Gad's Hill Place, Dickens's last home, in which he died. It is now used as a girls' school, but is usually open to visitors. This is the same Gadshill mentioned in Shakspere's *Henry IV* where Falstaff had his adventure with the " men in buckram," and at the Sir John Falstaff Tavern

we may obtain strength and sustenance in the form of good Kentish beer.

Then Rochester! A panorama of it lies before you as you descend from Gadshill. You cross the Medway, the castle commanding the view. It all looks very Dickensy.

Mr. Pickwick notes that the principal productions of Rochester are " soldiers, sailors, Jews, chalk, shrimps, officers, and dockyard men." It was still true at my last visit.

Yes, the Bull Hotel is still there — " Good house — nice beds — Wright's next house, dear — very dear — half-a-crown in the bill, if you look at the waiter — charge you more if you dine at a friend's than they would if you dined in the coffee-room — rum fellows — very." (Wright's Crown Inn is no more.)

Everything is " intact." There is the very staircase where Jingle was the recipient of Dr. Slammer's defiance. Is it intact? Does fact agree with fiction?

Recall that one of the famous " points " of the first edition in the original paper covers is that the plate " Dr. Slammer's Defiance of Mr. Jingle " (Plate IV in Part I) should, in its first state, show eleven boards on the floor, the floor being the resting stage of the grand staircase of the Bull Inn at Rochester. In spite

BULL HOTEL, ROCHESTER

"Do you remain here, Sir?" inquired Mr. Nathaniel Winkle.
"Here — not I — but you'd better — good house — nice beds —"

BALLROOM, BULL HOTEL, ROCHESTER

"It was a long room, with crimson-covered benches, and wax candles in glass chandeliers. The musicians were securely confined in an elevated den, and quadrilles were being systematically got

of the suspicion which will doubtless attach to us (from the eternally distrustful servants of an English inn, especially where Americans are concerned, and perhaps not unwarrantedly, to find an elderly gentleman on his knees examining the boards on the staircase), in spite of the controversy which will undoubtedly arise at the announcement of our conclusion, we shall count them. We did. They were seven.

The ballroom, equally " intact," corresponds exactly to the description:

" It was a long room, with crimson-covered benches, and wax candles in glass chandeliers. The musicians were securely confined in an elevated den, and quadrilles were being systematically got through by two or three sets of dancers. Two card-tables were made up in the adjoining card-room, and two pair of old ladies, and a corresponding number of stout gentlemen, were executing whist therein."

Because *Pickwick Papers* did not become popular until the appearance of Sam Weller, one might be led to suppose that the earlier chapters do not come up to the later standard of excellence. But this is a poor judgment. Mr. Jingle is colossal — as good in his way and as original as Sam Weller himself. It is a pity he ever reformed and became serious. But, then, nobody can quite believe in Dickens's reformations. All the

incidents at Rochester are exquisitely funny — for instance, Jingle's cool response to the infuriated Dr. Slammer when the latter presents his card:

" Ah! Slammer — much obliged — polite attention — not ill now, Slammer — but when I am — knock you up."

Also the duel, and the bloodthirsty second with the camp-stool!

The day after the ball was the day of the uncompleted duel, and the day after that was the day of the review. The Duke of Wellington, by the way, should have been the reviewing commander, but wasn't because he was temporarily " out," owing to some political differences. Here the Pickwickians met Mr. Wardle and his family and were invited to Dingley Dell.

Where is Dingley Dell? It is one of the few entirely fictitious spots in the entire book.

" Dingley Dell, gentlemen — fifteen miles, gentlemen " — the words of the waiter at the Bull are our only hint.

It can't be near Cobham — Cobham is a little village only five miles from Rochester, which does not correspond to the waiter's instructions, and, besides the discrepancy in distance, Cobham is specifically named in Chapter XI, for it was at the Leather Bottle there that after his disappointment in love the re-

union of Mr. Tupman with the other Pickwickians took place.

The whereabouts of Muggleton, whose cricket team

THE LEATHER BOTTLE, COBHAM

The lovesick Tupman surprised

opposed Dingley Dell, is also a matter of conjecture. If it is to any degree a portrait of any Kentish town, according to Charles Dickens the younger, Town

Malling sat for it, while van Noorden thinks the prob-
abilities point to Maidstone. That would be the other
side of Rochester from Cobham.

Dingley Dell is probably on the southern side of
Rochester also. When the Pickwickians leave Dingley
Dell to find Mr. Tupman, they go first to Muggleton,
take a conveyance to Rochester, and thence walk to
Cobham. All this seems to place Dingley Dell on the
other (southern) side of Rochester.

Cobtree, Sandling, is the spot selected by Mr. van
Noorden as the actual original of Dingley Dell. Mr.
Frost, an early student of the Dickens topography,
wrote as follows:

" Dingley Dell, if it is to be found at all, must be
sought . . . east of the Medway, between the two
lines of railway, and west of a curved line drawn from
Judd's Hill to Paddock Wood, through Otterden and
Staplehurst; and in that portion of Kent, though
there may be many spots the seclusion and pictur-
esqueness of which might suggest such a name as
Dingley Dell, there is no town to correspond to Muggleton. All the localities mentioned by Dickens in his
narrative of the Pickwickians' journey and their so-
journs at Manor Farm must be regarded, therefore,
as being equally with Mr. Wardle and the fat boy the
creations of his fancy."

Wherever it is, all the scenes in this locality have

charm — the familiar charm of the English countryside. Provided you have good weather, you could do
no better than walk yourself over the roads and along
the lanes of Kent and pick out your own Dingley Dell.

Dorking is visited more easily from Rochester than
any place else on the journey.

There is no sight which could warm the Pickwickian
heart so much as the Marquis of Granby, the public
house over which Mrs. Weller presided. We know it
was at Dorking: Dorking is today a small market
town, twenty-nine miles southwest of London, six
miles west of Reigate.

There is, however, little authentically Pickwickian
to see in Dorking. There is not now, nor ever was, a
Marquis of Granby, though there were many such
pubs in other parts of England. In the familiar scene
on the title-page showing Mr. Stiggins being doused
in front of the inn, the signboard portrays the Marquis himself in the uniform of a general officer.

The real Marquis, " of glorious memory," was the
eldest son of John, third Duke of Rutland, was Colonel of the Royal Regiment of the Horse Guards from
May 1758 to October 1770, served as second in command to Lord George Sackville at the Battle of Min-
den. " The Marquis' great popularity," we are told,
" both with the army and the people generally, no
doubt accounted for the fact of so many public houses

being named after him " (Jubilee Edition, *Pickwick*).

We have only two choices at Dorking, if we are determined to identify the Marquis of Granby — the King's Head and the King's Arms. G. A. Sala in *Household Words* mentioned the King's Head, " which by the way is the original of the ' Marquis of Granby.' " Dickens was editor of *Household Words* and by assumption read and found no disagreement with this statement. Mr. van Noorden, however, believes that King's Arms is more like the description of the " model of a roadside public house of the better class — just large enough to be convenient and small enough to be snug."

Since you are in the neighbourhood, you should go on to Canterbury, if you have never visited that ancient city. Another trip, of non-Pickwickian interest, from Rochester as a base, is to Knole, the manor house of the Sackvilles, and to my mind the most magnificent home of its kind in England. It is possessed of a beauty quite breath-taking. Portions of the interior are open to the public on certain days of the week and you should inquire as to this in London before you start, so that your visit to Rochester will fall upon one of these days. One can see Gads Hill, Rochester and Cobham and Knole in one day and go on to Canterbury to spend the next day there.

In Rochester itself, however, we have not yet men-

tioned the Cathedral. It is one of my favourites in
England. I like only Salisbury and Lincoln better.
The nave is one of the finest examples of Norman architecture in the world. The crypt is one of the
largest. And the coloured effigy of John of Sheppey,
Bishop of Rochester, who died in 1360, is evidently
referred to by Mr. Jingle. The tomb had been bricked
up and forgotten; it was discovered and revealed in
1825.

" '. . . Old cathedral too — earthly smell — pilgrims feet worn away the old steps — little Saxon
doors — confessionals like money-takers' boxes at
theatres — queer customers, those monks — Popes,
and Lord Treasurers,[1] and all sorts of old fellows,
with great red faces, and broken noses, turning up
every day . . . matchlocks — Sarcophagus — fine
place — old legends too — strange stories: capital ';
and the stranger continued to soliloquize until they
reached the Bull Inn, in the High street."

Among the famous bishops of Rochester was John
Fisher, beheaded because he refused to acknowledge
the Act of Supremacy, in 1535; he was canonized by
the Bishop of Rome last year, a proceeding which
shocked me deeply. So far as it was in the power of
any man to make a saint of John Fisher, his own acts
did so.

[1] John of Sheppy was Lord High Treasurer from 1358 to 1360.

Still another was Nicholas Ridley, who was burnt at Oxford in 1555. How the stout words of his companion martyr, Hugh Latimer, ring in the heart: " Play the man, Master Ridley; we shall this day light a candle by God's grace in England as I trust shall never be put out " !

For the Dickensian, Rochester and Rochester Cathedral, of course, are notable as the scenes of *Edwin Drood*. No other book of Dickens, ironically, has had so voluminous a literature gather about it. Ironically, because the truth is it is one of his worst books.

My friend Vincent Starrett is an ardent Droodian and has in his collection all the solutions of the mystery — heaven knows how many. I have quite a few myself, including that one published at Brattleboro, Vermont, in 1873, by a medium who claimed that the spirit pen of Charles Dickens had dictated the end of the unfinished work upon which he was working at the time of his death.

" By those who are acquainted with the principles of spiritualism, (and those who are not, can easily understand them by adopting Mr. Dickens' suggestions, as given in his Preface to this work), it will be easily understood that the first production of a spirit pen would be very liable to contain some imperfections; and more especially would that be the case, where both the medium and the spirit by whom he is

controlled, are lacking in experience, and consequently development, but I believe future works, which are to come from the spirit-pen of Mr. Dickens, will be entirely free from imperfections, even if any such exist in the present volume," says the author in his Preface.

He need not have worried. The spirit pen did just as well as Dickens himself in *Edwin Drood;* nothing could be any worse than the part he really wrote.

Nowhere on the journey did I miss my truant companions, Woollcott and Starrett, more than at Rochester. Woollcott, too, is a Droodian, and while I deprecate the lack of discrimination which allows these two connoisseurs to admire the book, their bickerings would have been amusing in Rochester Cathedral because Woollcott believes that Datchery was Helena Landless in disguise. Starrett adds waspishly that he also believes in Santa Claus, because Starrett holds to the perfectly sound theory that Datchery was Bazzard.

As a matter of cold fact, the wretched book isn't even a mystery. It is simply a sort of hero-worshipping awe that persuades Dickensians to regard it as such. Any five-year-old boy not actually the inmate of a home for the feeble-minded can solve it in a second. George Gissing was right — it is a " paltry mystery." Of course Edwin was murdered by Jasper.

Why would his ring be found else? The body was destroyed by quicklime. The apparition that appears to Jasper (see the cover) was probably (I cannot be

DORKING REVISITED

Snodgrass shows conclusively that Helena Landless could not have been Datchery.

dogmatic about this) Helena Landless dressed in Edwin's clothes. Datchery-Bazzard uncovers the plot and exposes the murder, after a chase, joined by Neville Landless, up the winding stairs. Of course.

Chesterton speaks somewhere of all the books being

merely strips cut from the flowing roll of Charles Dickens. And there are two distinct parts to them. One, for want of a better name, we can call " serious " and the other " comic." And since I have made such a crass characterization, we might as well continue in the same strain and say that the serious part is bad and the comic part is magnificent. There is hardly an exception — *A Tale of Two Cities* is a possible one — a serious part of Dickens that might be called good. As Dickens got older, the serious parts got longer and more predominant, so that few of the books after *Christmas Stories* are worth reading.

Edwin Drood is as bad as *Denis Duval* or *Daniel Deronda* or *Tess of the D'Urbervilles* or *The Professor* or *Lady Chatterley's Lover* — no, here I fall into exaggeration. Nothing is as bad as *Lady Chatterley's Lover*.

NORWICH, BURY ST. EDMUNDS, AND IPSWICH

The Pickwickians had determined to view at first hand a typical English election. " In a few days, an election is to take place for the borough of Eatanswill, at which Mr. Perker, a gentleman whom I have lately met, is an agent of one of the candidates. We will behold, and minutely examine, a scene so interesting to every Englishman."

So after engaging Mr. Samuel Weller as a personal attendant, and announcing in somewhat ambiguous terms this new aspect of his domestic affairs to Mrs. Bardell, the Pickwickians took the Norwich coach.

Their journeys, in the next chapters, were:

May 29 — Departed from London for Eatanswill (*Norwich* or *Sudbury*).

June 8 — Got wind of Jingle and traced him to *Bury St. Edmunds*.

Return to London.

September 5 — Mr. Weller senior put them on the trail of Jingle and Job Trotter again, so they followed them to *Ipswich*.

For us, their humble followers, these towns can be taken in one trip, especially if we go by motor.

The journey takes us to the northeast of England, a pleasant land. If we go by train we leave from Liverpool Street Station; a convenient train is at about 9 a.m. It is not feasible to make Norwich, Ipswich, Sudbury, and Bury St. Edmunds all in one day by train. Norwich and Ipswich are easily visited in one day, returning to London, and leaving the others for another trip.

The identity of Eatanswill is problematical. The text says:

" We will frankly acknowledge, that up to the period of our being first immersed in the voluminous

papers of the Pickwick club, we had never heard of Eatanswill; we will with equal candour admit, that we have in vain searched for proof of the actual exist- ence of such a place at the present day. . . . We are therefore led to believe, that Mr. Pickwick, with that anxious desire to abstain from giving offence to any, and with those delicate feelings for which all who knew him well know he was so eminently remarkable, pur- posely substituted a fictitious designation, for the real name of the place in which his observations were made. We are confirmed in this belief by a little circum- stance, apparently slight and trivial in itself, but when considered in this point of view, not undeserving of notice. In Mr. Pickwick's note-book, we can just trace an entry of the fact, that the places of himself and followers were booked by the Norwich coach; but this entry was afterwards lined through, as if for the purpose of concealing even the direction in which the borough is situated."

If they took the Norwich coach, is Norwich to be nominated as the real Eatanswill? Not necessarily, but there is no reason why it shouldn't.

Mr. van Noorden names Sudbury as the real Eat- answill. " Topographically, historically and logi- cally, Sudbury is the place. Granted there are inci- dents of the Ipswich election included in the account of that immortal struggle, even the most virulent op-

ponent of the Sudbury theory has now conceded the point."

I am not privy to the whereabouts of the controversy which became so virulent, so I am unable to recapitulate the arguments.

Fitzgerald's suggestion that Exeter was intended because Dickens " took " the speech of Lord John Russell there in 1835 is obviously refuted by the note that the Pickwickians took the Norwich coach, Exeter being in the exactly opposite direction.

Both Sudbury and Norwich, and, for that matter, Ipswich, would correspond to the statement in Chapter XV.

When Mr. Pickwick surprised Jingle at Mrs. Leo Hunter's garden party (of course at Eatanswill), Jingle dodges away always with a plausible excuse.

" ' Hallo! ' said Jingle. ' Quite forgot — no directions to postilion — give 'em at once — back in a minute.' "

Mr. Pickwick learned after his escape what Jingle's destination was to be: " At Bury St. Edmunds, not many miles from here."

From Sudbury, which is on the very southern border of Suffolk, to Bury St. Edmunds is, as a matter of fact, about thirty miles by road.

You can visit Bury St. Edmunds (the Borough of St. Edmund) from London and return in one day in

plenty of time for meeting friends at the cocktail hour, dinner, and the theatre. It is well worth it — a

BURY ST. EDMUNDS

What might have been. Clendening locates Westgate House for Pickwick and Snodgrass.

magnificent old city, quietly moving about its modest affairs, dreaming of its great past.

Once there was a martyrdom here, and royal blood was spattered upon this placid ground. King Edmund was killed by the arrows of the Danes. He be-

came St. Edmund — hence the curious name — and his grave was a shrine, where miracles were performed. Strange that in this matter-of-fact-looking countryside water was turned to wine, and the lame were healed, and the blind made to see. But so 'tis said it was and folk flocked from all parts of England to see these wonders. It became a great and prosperous place then, with an abbey and two fairs.

Only some ruins of that abbey remain, as of all those great establishments — Beaulieu, Netley near Southampton, Glastonbury in the west, and Fountains and Whitby in the north. Oh, the purpled abbots! you muse as you walk through the lush gardens of Fountains Abbey — how well they knew how to pick their spots! Their ghosts must haunt those desecrated shrines — they could never be happy in any heaven.

There is only one fair now — held, they say, in December. The other was abolished by the " Act " of 1871. There it is — sullen socialism ruining Merrie England.

There is also Westgate House, the scene of Mr. Pickwick's adventure at the girls' boarding school.

While the taxi-driver sullenly smoked a social cigarette, I explained to an imaginary audience, composed of Woollcott and Starrett, the reasons for the

identification, with a few remarks on the decline and fall of East Anglia.

Norwich, the capital of East Anglia, is a noble city. It was the home of Sir Thomas Browne, whose memory is preserved by a fine statue in the market place.

Here also is the house where George Borrow was born, with a modest plaque upon the wall near the door.

There is a gem of a cathedral — Nurse Edith Cavell's simple grave in Life's Green just under the walls.

Robert Green, Shakspere's vituperator, and John Crome the artist, Horatio Nelson, and James Martineau were all associated with Norwich.

The antiquities include Tombland, which has nothing to do with tombs, but derives from the old word " toom," or wasteland, at the monastery gates; Suckling House; and the beautiful Dolphin Inn (1587).

A visit to Norwich would be worth while if for no other reason than that the public-spirited citizens of Norwich put on the map to the east of Norwich the magic words " Dickens Land." Which means, I take it, that Yarmouth was the home of the Peggottys in *David Copperfield*.

With all these advantages, it is best, if you have to make a choice between visiting Sudbury and Norwich,

to assume that you do not agree with the vituperative adherents of the Sudbury theory, and that it was at Norwich that the Eatanswill election was held.

It is true that at Sudbury they will show you an inn which corresponds to the Town Arms Inn, the headquarters of the Blue interests, and the very platform where the fat town crier proclaimed silence so that the election proceedings could proceed.

One wonders, as one reads of the Eatanswill election, whether it is supposed to be a description of an election before the Reform Bill or afterwards. Was Eatanswill a rotten borough?

The dates here are confusing. The Reform Bill, which disenfranchised the rotten boroughs and redistributed parliamentary seats according to units of population, was passed on the 7th of May 1832. *Pickwick*, as we know, was actually written in 1836. The events which it purports to describe, however, are fictionally dated about 1827. But Dickens was careless (let us say Pickwickian) in other places as to anachronisms. He himself even put in a footnote in Chapter II saying that Mr. Jingle's reference to the revolution of July was a remarkable instance of the prophetic force of his imagination: the dialogue occurred in 1827, the revolution in 1830.

Dickens was born in 1812, learned shorthand, and became a parliamentary reporter at the age of seven-

teen, which would be in 1829 or 1830. The only country election which we have a record of his reporting was that in Exeter in 1835.[1] It was probably still fresh in his mind when he wrote the description of Eatanswill.

He never himself apparently was the eyewitness of an election in pre-Reform days, but this, of course, does not preclude the possibility that he could have described it from accounts or from historical records.

The Eatanswill election *could* have been, so far as the description gives us any evidence, either before or after Reform — in communities of any size the habits of the political parties were not changed by the passage of the bill.

The story Sam tells of his father's adventure when he drove a coachful of voters from London to a country district for one party and upset his coach and turned every man into the canal for the other party has an actual historical basis (at an election in the very corrupt borough of Great Yarmouth).

[1] "The very last time I was at Exeter, I strolled into the castle yard there to identify for the amusement of a friend the spot on which I once 'took,' as we used to call it, an election speech of Lord John Russell, at the Devon contest, in the midst of a lively fight by all the vagabonds in that division of the county, and under such a pelting rain that I remember two good natured colleagues who chanced to be at leisure held a pocket handkerchief over my note-book after the manner of a state canopy in an ecclesiastical procession." — From a speech made by Dickens at the annual dinner of the Newspaper Press Fund, May 1865.

We have every evidence that the elections as conducted in those days would have made the late Senator from Louisiana jealous if he had ever heard of them. Every sort of trick was used to win them. Parties brought electors from outside into a contested district. They bribed and cajoled and influenced properly qualified voters. They " eliminated," in one way or another, voters of the other party. Sam Weller's own description is an example of one form of elimination:

" ' Fine, fresh, hearty fellows they seem,' said Mr. Pickwick, glancing from the window.

" ' Werry fresh,' replied Sam; ' me, and the two waiters at the Peacock, has been a pumpin' over the independent woters as supped there last night.'

" ' Pumping over independent voters ! ' exclaimed Mr. Pickwick.

" ' Yes,' said his attendant, ' every man slept vere he fell down; we dragged 'em out, one by one, this mornin', and put 'em under the pump, and they're in reg'lar fine order, now. Shillin' a head the committee paid for that 'ere job.'

" ' Can such things be ! ' exclaimed the astonished Mr. Pickwick.

" ' Lord bless your heart, Sir,' said Sam, ' why, where was you half baptized? — that's nothin', that a'nt.'

" ' Nothing? said Mr. Pickwick.

" ' Nothin' at all, Sir,' replied his attendant. ' The night afore the last day o' the last election here, the opposite party bribed the bar-maid at the Town Arms, to hocus the brandy and water of fourteen un-polled electors as was a stoppin' in the house.'

" ' What do you mean by " hocussing " brandy and water? ' inquired Mr. Pickwick.

" ' Puttin' laud'num in it,' replied Sam. ' Blessed if she didn't send 'em all to sleep till twelve hours arter the election was over. They took one man up to the booth, in a truck, fast asleep, by way of experiment, but it was no go — they wouldn't poll him; so they brought him back, and put him to bed again.' "

In many of the boroughs before Reform the entire electorate was bribed. They felt no shame at this cor-ruption, but had come to look on the franchise merely as an opportunity to get an annual dinner and sep-tennial bribe. One of Sheridan's constituents said to him about the low cost of votes: " Oh, sir, things can-not go on this way! There must be a reform. We poor electors are not properly paid at all."

In the borough of Shoreham the voters actually formed a union, which was called the Christian Club, in order to obtain the most money and make the best bargain for a solid vote.

Violence was a regular feature of an election. After

a Brentford election a witness testified as follows: "Atkinson Bush maketh oath that he was at Brentford on the day of the election, and seeing a large body of men with labels in their hats, whereon was written, 'Proctor and Liberty,' this deponent asked them whether they were all voters for Proctor? Upon which they declared they had no votes, but had in their hands what was as good, and showed him their bludgeons; and being asked who they supposed would get the election, they replied, Proctor, swearing if Glynn got the advantage, 'By G——, we will have his blood!'"

Plug-uglies were regularly employed, and Broughton, the famous pugilist, was much in demand at election time.

One instance of a young man whose skull was fractured by a blow from a bludgeon was the subject of a caricature on the College of Surgeons. The actual circumstances were that after his death the College sat secretly and decided that the blow was not the cause of the young man's death. The caricature shows the surgeons in consultation. The president, holding up a money-bag, says: "This convinces me that Clarke did not die of the wound he received at Brentford." A Scotch surgeon remarks: "By my Soul, his head was too thick to be broken, or he would ne'er ha'

gang'd to Brentford." A third, glancing enviously at the money, says: " Another such bag would convince me Clarke never received any blow."

To show how little things were changed by the passage of the Reform Bill we have a record of an election at Coventry in 1837, where two thousand roughs were engaged as bullies to intimidate all who wanted to vote against the Liberal candidates. They received five shillings a day and had orders to " beat the electors roundly and leave them alive, but hardly." One of them later said: " Whenever I saw any of the voters near the booths, I dragged them by the hair. . . . We kicked and beat them as long as we liked, and then the constables came and took them away; they dared not interfere before." [1]

We may reasonably conclude then that Dickens's picture of the Eatanswill election was not overdrawn. His account and Hogarth's pictures remain as the best contemporary records of those scenes.

But far more important than the election was Mrs. Leo Hunter's garden party at The Den, Eatanswill.

In M. Maurois's little study of Dickens he describes a scene which he says is often to be observed in Eng-

[1] A full and interesting account of these malpractices will be found in the book *How the World Votes,* by Charles Seymour and Donald Paige Frary. Springfield, Massachusetts: C. A. Nichols Company; 1918.

lish music halls, especially in the provinces: the actor
is announced as a Dickens impersonator and solicits
votes from the audience for the character they wish
impersonated. The cry goes up: " Micawber," and
Micawber he does. Then Sir Mulberry Hawk, and
Pecksniff, and so on. And M. Maurois reflects on the
impossibility of such a situation anywhere else on
earth for any other author. Could it happen in France
for Balzac, in Russia for Dostoievsky, or in America
for Hawthorne?

I have never been lucky enough to witness such a
performance, but we came near it at The Den in
Eatanswill.

My wife and I ruthlessly threw historical principles to the winds (of which there are many on the
eastern coast of England in the summer) and definitely identified The Den in Norwich.

It had been our intention that my wife would im-
personate Mrs. Leo Hunter on the steps of the town
hall and there recite the " Ode to an Expiring Frog."
But we had underestimated the density of the throngs
which move up and down the streets of the capital of
East Anglia. The lady declined.

But in the quiet lane around The Den conditions
seemed ideal. The moving-picture camera was set up,
my wife put on the helmet (especially procured in
London and constituting our only piece of luggage

on the Norwich trip) of Mrs. Leo Hunter, and in a
quavering voice recited the immortal lines:

" Can I view thee panting, lying . . ."

My wife's voice, when nervous, has a carrying quality. The lane had been completely deserted when she
began, but at the first syllable two figures appeared
round the corner, with the suddenness of popped
grains of corn. Strays began moving in, and when
they beheld the helmet they motioned wildly and the
shock troops came on a run.

The movie machine got jammed and the impersona-
tor of Mrs. Leo Hunter had to start all over again.
The audience, densely packed, awaited breathlessly.
This time the line:

" On thy stomach, without sighing,"

brought a faint cheer. Emboldened by this encourage-
ment, she brought on the lines

" On a log,
Expiring frog!" [1]

with great feeling.

" Say," she said suddenly, going up a full octave.
I feared she was about to launch into the " Star-
Spangled Banner " or to confirm the Englishman's
fixed belief that all Americans begin all their sentences
in that fashion.

[1] Dear old Augustine Birrell selected them as the motto for
his final volume, *Et Cetera.*

" Say, have fiends in shape of boys,"

went on the brave voice.

The heads of fiends in shape of boys, and fiends in shape of little girls, appeared over the tops of walls, crawled through fences, dropped from the boughs of trees. As we said afterwards, the only trouble with birth-control is that it has come too late.

They pressed about us,

" With wild halloo and brutal noise."

The situation was threatening. Our taxi-driver stationed at one approach did yeoman service by tapping his forehead and saying the single magic words: " Americans." This, however, controlled only part of the crowd.

But Mrs. Leo Hunter pushed on until the peroration:

" With a dog,
        Expiring frog! "

She had finished. She looked at me imploringly and we peered apprehensively around for a road of escape. The crowd was milling and muttering hoarsely. Just then a constable heaved into sight. And what a constable! He might have stepped from any English detective novel. He had a note-book; he frowned. He said: " Wot's this all abaht? "

Things looked bad. We have never spent the night in an English jail, and we did not wish to be taken to the station-house for questioning. The thing also, it must be admitted, did not look just queer; it looked downright suspicious. Sedition seemed to be the least grave of the charges that could be preferred against us. We knew the procedure full well: had we patronized the only intelligent department of English literature for the last six decades in vain? Scotland Yard would be summoned, and the C.I.D. would send one of its crack men straightway.

With the sweetest of smiles, my wife decided that honesty is the best policy.

" I have been reciting Mrs. Leo Hunter's ' Ode to an Expiring Frog,' " she said. " The lane seemed empty when we began."

The words fell upon the sullen throng like drops of glistening cool dew. Nothing could have been braver, more innocent, more childlike, nor more desperate. I admired her then, but I cursed the mad folly of this idiotic-sounding explanation. As I glanced over the faces of the crowd, however, I saw a change, a look of comprehension.

The constable pushed back his cap and smiled.

" 'Fraid we couldn't understand the accent, sir," he said.

" I do readings from *Pickwick* myself, sir," he

added. " The trial scene, you know, from the author's prepared stige directions."

" Yore best is Bill Sikes and Nawncy, though, Sam," ventured an ancient.

" Won't you do it now for us? " asked my companion with sugared tones.

" Not in uniform, miss," replied the constable. When the " miss " came out I could see the C.I.D.'s elimination.

" Sharp's here," said a voice. " He'll do Old Joe Bagstock."

He did, with great gusto.

We had Dick Swiveller and the Marchioness after that, from a very small, thin, dirty little boy, and then Wilkins Micawber, from a very large, fat, dirty old man, and then the discomfiture of Uriah Heep, and then — well, more were offered but we made our excuses, distributed a small sum to be used after closing time was over, and, seeking the seclusion that the taxi granted, we drove triumphantly away.

" What," inquired my wife — removing the somewhat dilapidated papier-mâché helmet of Mrs. Leo Hunter and replacing it with the hat she had bought at Schiaparelli's, when the escape was complete — " do we do now? "

" We go on to Ipswich," was my proposal. " Something tells me closing time will soon be over and we

will be just set to obtain one of those warm muck-like beverages the British call ' veesky-soda.' "

Ipswich is notable in the Pickwickian sense for the Great White Horse Inn (Chapters XXII to XXV), where Mr. Pickwick got lost, entered the wrong bed-room, and found too late that it was occupied also by the lady in the yellow curl-papers.

The Great White Horse still stands, still " rendered . . . conspicuous by a stone statue of some rampacious animal with flowing mane and tail, distantly resembling an inane cart-horse, which is elevated above the principal door."

The inn itself, as every visitor avers, corresponds exactly to Dickens's description: " Never were such labyrinths of uncarpeted passages, such clusters of mouldy, badly-lighted rooms, such huge numbers of small dens for eating or sleeping in, beneath any one roof, as are collected together between the four walls of the Great White Horse at Ipswich."

No wonder, as everyone says delightedly, Mr. Pickwick got lost. The famous adventure, which consisted merely of being found in a lady's bedroom, seems pallid in these days of lusty fornication in novels, but in the prim days of 1836 it seemed exquisitely embarrassing.

They show you at the Great White Horse the very room where the adventure of the lady with the yellow

curl-papers occurred. It is No. 36 and is invested with
every verisimilitude. " There were the two beds, whose
situation he perfectly remembered, and the fire still
burning."

If you ask the page-boy whether you can inspect
the room, he says : " Oh, yes, sir — this way, sir," with
a sort of sixpence alacrity.

When you ask his name he says something that
sounds like " Villum, sir," which startles you.

" William what? " you ask.

" Just Villum, sir."

And it turns out that he calls himself by his last
name, which is *Wilhum*. You ask him if he would like
to be in a book and it is his turn to look startled, but
he manages to say : " Yes, sir," politely, and that's
that.

The room comes up to all expectations. There are
the two beds and the fireplace and there has been
added a very modern wash-stand.

You ask Wilhum whether many come to see the
room.

" Yes, sir," he answers, and sadly adds : " Mostly
Amedicans, sir. It's curious how much more interested
Amedicans are than English to see it."

" There was a lady and gentleman from Philadelphia spent the night there last week — just for the

THE GREAT WHITE HORSE HOTEL,
IPSWICH

THE PICKWICK BEDROOM
The Great White Horse Hotel, Ipswich

experience," he contributes on receipt of the sixpence. " Ever hear of Philadelphia, sir? "

Which query rates him an extra shilling.

But these acknowledgments of the realism of the great novelist pale in comparison with the statements made in the old days when Murray's Handbook said that at the White Horse " occurred [*occurred*, mind you, not *is placed* by the imagination of the novelist] Mr. Pickwick's remarkable adventure with the lady in the yellow curl papers. One traveller asked the landlord whether it were not the hotel where Mr. Pickwick was supposed to have put up. ' Supposed,' he exclaimed, ' I have the very knife and fork he used when he was here; ivory mounted, they are; they go with the hotel and were handed to me when I took it."

The inns of *Pickwick* are many in number. Here is a list of them which I think is complete:

1. The Golden Cross, Charing Cross
*2. The Bull, Rochester
3. The Bull, Whitechapel
4. The Blue Lion, Muggleton
5. The White Hart, Boro'
*6. The Old Leather Bottle, Cobham
7. The George and Vulture, Lombard Street
8. The Town Arms, Eatanswill
9. The Peacock, Eatanswill

*10. The Angel, Bury St. Edmunds

11. The White Hart, Bath (now the Grand Pump Room Hotel)

12. The Bush, Bristol

*13. The Great White Horse, Ipswich

*14. The Spaniards, Hampstead

15. The Fox under the Hill, Adelphi

16. The Magpie and Stump, London

17. The Markis o' Granby, Dorking

*18. The Bell, Berkeley Heath

*19. The Hop Pole, Tewkesbury

20. The old Royal Hotel, Birmingham

*21. The Saracen's Head, Towcester (now the Pomfret Arms)

*22. Osborne's Hotel, Adelphi

Those starred can still be visited.

What about these inns? What of their hospitality — their present-day comfort?

It was customary, not long ago, to sigh for the glories of the past and long for the good old coaching days and the stop by the roadside at mine inn, to take mine ease. When automobiles came in, they made this dream come true, and we can sample now the pleasures of the inns our fathers praised in the coaching days.

If you are longing for past comforts, you may stop that and thank your stars you are living in our time.

In our modern age there may not be many desirable things, but there is more comfort to the square inch than there ever was before in the history of the world. Other ages may have had more leisure, more time to contemplate life, more genius, better conversation, more abundant life, but for making the old bag of bones perfectly happy this present period cannot be even faintly approached.

Sentimental dreams of the delights of a round of visits to quaint coaching inns in England are purely visionary. The actual fact is that outside of London, and only a selected part of that, and a few other cities (Bath, Edinburgh, Glasgow, Birmingham, Liverpool), the great achievements of civilization in the direction of personal comfort, so far as the English are concerned, might as well never have been made. In a country where you are constantly numbed by a kind of clammy, " penithrating " cold, a furnace is a luxury, a district rarity. Modern bathroom facilities, even a water-closet, are regarded as effeminate.

Contrary to the usual opinion, the food in the countryside in England is better than in France, and the service in France better than in England. Outside the capitals, I mean — Paris and London are level in both: I see no marked superiority in the Parisian cuisine. Swedish cooking, for that matter, is better than either.

BATH, BRISTOL, AND ENVIRONS

" Oh Sammy, Sammy, vy worn't there a alleybi! "

With these tragic words echoing in his heart, Mr. Samuel Weller concluded the affair of Bardell versus Pickwick.

But there was no alibi. The case went against Mr. Pickwick. He determined to refuse to pay the costs and in the course of time he is to go to the Fleet Prison, where he is to meet the Zephyr, and Mr. Smangle, and Mr. Mivens.

From Mr. Weller, who thinks Mr. Pickwick's principles are too strict, he hears about the man who killed himself on principle. That story was taken from Boswell, an anecdote by Mr. Beauclerk about " ' Mr. —— , who loved buttered muffins, but durst not eat them because they disagreed with his stomach,' and who resolved to shoot himself in consequence, carrying out his resolution after eating three buttered muffins, ' knowing that he should not be troubled with indigestion.' "

I have always liked that story. In fact, I intend to emulate the gentleman one of these days, because a very tragic thing has occurred to me. I have become a victim of the gout. But just before I had my first attack I ordered some Burgundy — Romanée Conti 1929, and it has been in my cellar ever since. I can't

bear to let anybody else drink it and if I drink it myself I am sure to have the gout. So one of these days
I intend to drink all of it I want to and then emulate
the gentleman of the buttered muffins.

Yes, on principle, Mr. Pickwick had all the excite-
ment of the Fleet before him. As Chesterton says,
there is a phrase about being taken in — the wise and
the cynical and the crafty are never taken in by life,
but those with childlike hearts like Mr. Pickwick are.
The Fleet Prison opens its doors, and with torches
and banners and drums he is taken in. Taken in to
find a new set of adventures and to see a new world.

But even without knowing the experiences in store
for him, the prospect of incarceration did not dismay
him. " I shall employ myself as usual, until the opposite party have the power of issuing a legal process
of execution against me."

" ' They can issue execution, my dear Sir . . .
next term,' replied Perker, ' just two months hence,
my dear Sir.'

" ' Very good,' said Mr. Pickwick. ' Until that
time, my dear fellow, let me hear no more of the matter. And now,' continued Mr. Pickwick, looking round
on his friends with a good-humoured smile, and a
sparkle in the eye which no spectacles could dim or
conceal, ' the only question is, Where shall we go to
next? ' "

Up spoke Mr. Winkle. " If you leave me to suggest our destination, I say Bath. I think none of us have ever been there."

What better reason could there be for going anywhere?

And so we are committed to follow them, and a very pleasant journey it will be.

Bath is, I think, after London, the most charming city in England. It still retains its air. It is pure eighteenth century. Every Bathian in conversation finishes his sentences just as did eighteenth-century people. Woollcott does the same thing — an astonishing habit.

Mr. Pickwick put up at Bath at the White Hart Hotel, opposite the Great Pump Room, but this has been replaced by the Grand Pump Room Hotel. On the outer wall of the latter is a plaque which commemorates the fact that Moses and Eleazer Pickwick owned the White Hart Hotel which was once on that site; they also owned the Bath-to-London stage-coach route, which explains the perturbation of Sam Weller in Chapter XXXV:

" ' Well, Sam,' said Mr. Pickwick, ' what's the matter now? '

" ' Here's rayther a rum go, Sir,' replied Sam.

" ' What? " inquired Mr. Pickwick.

BRONZE PLAQUE ON THE GRAND PUMP
ROOM HOTEL, BATH

The Origin of Bath.

Bladud, the son of a British king, was a leper, and for that reason was expelled from his father's Palace. Becoming a swineherd, his pigs were infected with the leprosy, but by rolling themselves in the warm mud through which they had to pass in their wanderings, they were soon cured. Bladud was eventually discovered taking his morning dip by two of the king's courtiers, who promptly took him home to his father. When he afterwards became king, he built the city of Bath B.C. 863 upon the muddy swamps which had proved so salutary to him.

ORIGIN OF BATH—THE LEGEND OF
PRINCE BLADUD

"*For many hundred years before that time, there had been handed down from age to age, an old legend, that the illustrious Prince being afflicted with leprosy, on his return from reaping a rich harvest of knowledge in ancient Athens, shunned the court of his royal father, and consorted moodily with husbandmen and pigs. Among the herd (so said the legend) was a pig of grave and solemn countenance, with whom the Prince had a fellow feeling — for he too was wise — a pig of thoughtful and reserved demeanour; an animal superior to his fellows, whose grunt was terrible, and whose bite was sharp. The young Prince sighed deeply as he looked upon the countenance of the majestic swine; — he thought of his royal father, and his eyes were bedewed with tears.*

"*This sagacious pig was fond of bathing in rich, moist mud. Not in summer as common pigs do now, to cool themselves . . . but in the cold sharp days of winter. His coat was ever so sleek, and his complexion so clear, that the Prince resolved to essay the purifying qualities of the same water that his friend resorted to. He made the trial. Beneath that black mud bubbled the hot springs of Bath. He washed, and was cured. Hastening to his father's court, he paid his best respects, and returning quickly hither, founded this city, and its famous baths.*"

" ' This here, Sir,' rejoined Sam. ' I'm wery much afeerd, Sir, that the properiator o' this here coach is a playin' some imperence vith us.'

" ' How is that, Sam? ' said Mr. Pickwick; ' aren't the names down on the way-bill? '

" ' The names is not only down on the vay-bill, Sir,' replied Sam, ' but they've painted vun on 'em up, on the door o' the coach.' As Sam spoke, he pointed to that part of the coach door on which the proprietor's name usually appears; and there sure enough, in gilt letters of a goodly size, was the magic name of PICK-WICK!

" ' Dear me,' exclaimed Mr. Pickwick, quite staggered by the coincidence; ' what a very extraordinary thing! '

" ' Yes, but that ain't all,' said Sam, again directing his master's attention to the coach door; ' not content vith writin' up Pickwick, they puts " Moses " afore it, vich I call addin' insult to injury, as the parrot said ven they not only took him from his native land, but made him talk the English langvidge arter-vards.'

" ' It's odd enough, certainly, Sam,' said Mr. Pickwick; ' but if we stand talking here, we shall lose our places.'

" ' Wot, ain't nothin' to be done in consequence,

Sir?' exclaimed Sam, perfectly aghast at the coolness with which Mr. Pickwick prepared to ensconce himself inside.

" 'Done!' said Mr. Pickwick. 'What should be done?'

" ' Ain't nobody to be whopped for takin' this here liberty, Sir?' said Mr. Weller, who had expected that at least he would have been commissioned to challenge the guard and coachman to a pugilistic encounter on the spot.

" ' Certainly not,' replied Mr. Pickwick eagerly; ' not on any account. Jump up to your seat directly.'

" ' I'm wery much afeerd,' muttered Sam to himself, as he turned away, ' that somethin' queer's come over the governor, or he'd never ha' stood this so quiet. I hope that 'ere trial hasn't broken his spirit, but it looks bad: wery bad.' Mr. Weller shook his head gravely; and it is worthy of remark, as an illustration of the manner in which he took this circumstance to heart, that he did not speak another word until the coach reached the Kensington turnpike, which was so long a time for him to remain taciturn, that the fact may be considered wholly unprecedented."

As we have mentioned, Dickens was in the west of England and visited Bath and Bristol in 1835, the year before the book was started. Undoubtedly he saw the name **Pickwick** on the stage-coach, and as so often

happens with names one sees on signboards, it tickled his risibilities. He used it at the first available opportunity.

In the Dickens House in London is an old signboard, recovered from Bath, labelled: " Pickwick Mews."

Not far from Bath is the village of Pickwick, although Dickens makes no mention of it.

Mr. Pickwick's stay at Bath corresponded to the very last stage of that Bath atmosphere which has been described by Smollett and Sheridan and Jane Austen.

Mr. Angelo Cyrus Bantam, Master of Ceremonies, must have been almost the last of that line of funtionaries. After Beau Nash died, in 1761, he was succeeded by one Samuel Derrick, then by Captain Wade, and then Major William Brereton. After that the record is somewhat confused, so it is not possible to identify Mr. Angelo Cyrus Bantam.

The food at the Grand Pump Room Hotel is, after London, the best food in England, and the wine excellent. It rained the first two days of our stay in Bath and we sat in our little room, with the coal fire crackling, reading the annals of the city, as comfortable as anyone could wish. Out of our window we could see Bath Abbey, with the chairmen sitting inside their chairs disconsolately, with the hoods up.

In Pickwick itself, in Chapter **XXXV**, there is the story of the origins of Bath according to the legend. Prince Bladud is encountered on many postcards, such as the one shown in the appended illustration.

One can find all the scenes mentioned in the book: the Royal Crescent, still magnificent — " perhaps the finest Crescent in Europe," according to the guide-book — the Circus, with its three rows of columns — Doric, Ionic, and Corinthian — Queen's Square, in which neighbourhood the famous Swarry must have been held.

" Turning now to Bath," writes van Noorden, " the scene of the ' Swarry ' is a much discussed item. It has been asserted that the Beaufort Arms, a little public house, is the place, because it was standing at the time (which I rather doubt), and because it was a resort of the Bath footmen.

" Now, why they should contradict the editor of the Pickwick Papers when he says — and he should know — that the Swarry was held at the home of Mr. Harris the Greengrocer, who was sometimes called in to assist (as greengrocers were and are) in the waiting, when a large party was on.

" He also records that the punch and other drinks were sent out for, which would not be the case if the ' Swarry ' were held at a tavern."

You enter Queen's Square the way of Sam Weller's

stroll — along Quiet Street. It must have been by
Quiet Street. You will be impelled to find Park Street,
which " was very much like the perpendicular streets
a man sees in a dream, which he cannot get up for the
life of him," and you will be rewarded because it is so
exactly like that.

Everywhere you go, you find memorial plaques on
the houses telling you of the famous people who lived
in Bath. The list of names which is hung in the lobby
of the hotel sounds like a roster of eighteenth-century
English literature, art, and drama.

Yes, it was a brilliant — really brilliant, in the true
sense of that abused word — a brilliant, gay time, the
like of which will never come again. The wit cracked
all the louder, the brittle laughter rattled all the
noisier, in that dead calm before the 9th Thermidor.
People of just that sort have never laughed since,
mainly because people of just that sort have not existed since.

Curious that it has not been pictured more often in
modern historical fiction. Still more curious that the
audacious figure of Beau Nash has not been the subject of one of the innumerable " modern " biogra-
phies. Lewis Melville has written a very dull sketch
of him. Goldsmith's *Life*, in spite of its old-fashioned
biographical circumlocutionary start, finally manages to catch the sparkle, perhaps because Goldsmith

was a fop himself. The only place I can recall where he appears in fiction is in *Monsieur Beaucaire*. Certainly he could have wished no more charming memorial.

The portrait Booth Tarkington draws of the great Beau is unflattering, but from all accounts quite fair. His parentage was uncertain, his preparation for life a complete failure. He went up to Oxford, but did not take his degree; whether he was sent down or, anticipating the inevitable, voluntarily decamped he never told. He then entered the army, but found the uniforms the only part of the regulations he could understand. The law next attracted his attention and he entered the Middle Temple. Here he cut a magnificent figure. He was known to be without funds and his fellow students thought he must be a highwayman in the leisure hours he could spare from the neglect of his studies.

Such romantic speculations missed the truth; he neither stole nor worked; he played for a living. He was a natural gambler. He would take a wager on anything. He bet that he would ride naked on a cow through a village high street, that he would stand clothed only in a blanket before the doors of York Minster as the congregation was leaving on Sunday morning. He anticipated the life of John Mytton, except that he had no fortune to dissipate.

He appeared in Bath in 1705, when he was about thirty years old. It was a time when the watering-places were becoming centres of fashion and he seized his opportunity with truly imperial command. Although Queen Anne had paid a visit to Bath and praised its waters, it had in 1705 none of the airs of a resort of fashion. The only notable building in the city was the Abbey. The baths had fallen into mire. There were no accommodations, no elegant houses. The lodgings and the streets were alike mean and dirty. There was no meeting-place for the *haut monde* — no ballroom, no gaming-rooms, no assembly-room, no theatre.

Worst of all, there was no etiquette.

Nash went about to change all that. And it must be said of him that he did it with great vigour and shrewdness. He started where everything should start, with a good band. He arranged a house for an assembly-room. He raised funds to provide proper facilities for enjoying the waters. He secured eighteen thousand pounds for good roads from London and for the environs. A theatre, a pump-room, and a permanent assembly-room were built under his direction.

Best of all, he provided a routine program of amusements. There were certain hours at which one did things — drank the waters, danced or gambled in the rooms, attended divine service, flirted, dined, gos-

siped, slept. He drew up a code of rules for conduct, which were rigidly enforced. The Beau himself not infrequently undertook the enforcement. On one occasion, hearing a young gallant address a lady in terms which he considered unsuited to the proprieties of his city, he laid hands upon him and threw him, clothes and all, into the waters of the bath. Nor did his disciplinary measures confine themselves to the gentlemen alone: when Katherine Hyde, Duchess of Queensbury, appeared at a dance wearing an apron, which ladies were supposed to wear only in the morning, he tore it off and threw it away. He issued regulations against duelling and the wearing of boots. He improved the manners of the bath-chairmen and regulated the charges of exorbitant lodging-keepers.

His own costume was unique among his subjects and gave semblance to his unwritten authority. He wore an immense white hat, coat and breeches gaudily emblazoned, and drove a chariot with six grey horses, and lackeys in laces, with French horns.

His state was maintained at first by a percentage of the profits from the gaming-tables. But this was stopped by laws against games of chance in 1745. The success of Bath was by that time so well established that the Beau was disregarded and neglected. His circumstances finally became so desperate that the corporation made him a small allowance. He had the

PARK STREET, BATH

*"Park Street was very much like the perpendicular streets a man
sees in a dream, which he cannot get up for the life of him."*

QUIET STREET, BATH,

*through which Sam Weller must have "walked with great delibera-
tion to Queen Square."*

misfortune to live to a very old age, embittered and railing against the ingratitude of man.

Arbiter elegantiarum though he was, he was not a wit. Perhaps even that is an understatement. There is the famous quip a man of my own profession made upon him, Dr. George Cheyne. The doctor was sitting with a group of jolly companions when he observed the pompous Beau approaching. " Gentlemen," he said to his friends, " let us still our mirth. Let us propose no more jokes or nonsense. Let us talk solemnities. Here comes a fool."

Goldsmith ascribes that to Locke, in which case it still remains in the medical profession.

If one or two other surviving anecdotes are to be believed, however, Cheyne did not always come off best in their encounters. The doctor asked the Beau once if he had followed his prescription. " Followed your prescription? " cried Nash. " No. Egad if I had, I should have broken my neck, for I flung it out of the third-storey window."

He was wont to ridicule the doctor's famous vegetable diet by calling it " Nebuchadnezzar," and vowed his design was to set the whole world grazing.

Bath being, of course, a health resort, it should be expected that among its citizens would be some distinguished physicians.

Not far from Bath lived an associate of its medical

men, a familiar in its streets — indeed, one of the greatest physicians of all, Edward Jenner, the proponent of vaccination against smallpox. He was born and practised at Berkeley, which is about twenty-five miles, as the crow flies, from Bath. At the Bell on Berkeley Heath the Pickwickians lunched on the way to Birmingham, where they were going to interview Mr. Winkle's father.

It was one of the dreams of my life to see that historic spot where vaccination was first performed, so we went to Berkeley (by bus to Bristol, and then changing to the Gloucester bus, which stops at Berkeley).

I referred above to Jenner's associations with the Bath physicians. In the Abbey it is not difficult to find the memorial to Caleb Hillier Parry, M.D., and in the Circus is a house with a plaque announcing it to have been the home of Caleb Hillier Parry. Parry's fame was restored to its rightful place by William Osler. A disease, exophthalmic goitre, so well known and prevalent now, was described in the earlier part of the nineteenth century by three men: Graves of Dublin, Basedow of Merseburg, and Flajani, an Italian. In the British Isles the disease is usually referred to as " Graves' disease," in Germany as " Basedow's disease," and in Italy as " Flajani's disease."

Osler, in his famous text-book on medicine, said: " In the posthumous writings of Caleb Hillier Parry (1825) is a description of 8 cases of Enlargement of the Thyroid Gland in connection with Enlargement or Palpitation of the Heart. In the first case, seen in 1786, he also described the exophthalmos. . . . If the name of any physician is to be associated with the disease, undoubtedly it should be that of the distinguished old Bath physician."

Jenner dedicated his *Inquiry*, one of the most influential books in medicine, to Dr. Parry. They were fast friends. When Jenner was ill with typhus fever, Parry came over from Bath to attend and nurse him. Parry, in his turn, dedicated a book to Jenner: *Cases of Tetanus and Rabies Contagiosa or Canine Hydrophobia* (Bath, 1814).

In an earlier day the most celebrated of the Bath physicians was George Cheyne, mentioned above. He wrote one of the first treatises on diet. He was a man of enormous bulk, who, like most dietitians, took very little of his own advice. He recorded the fascinating case of Colonel Townshend, who was able to make his heart stand still at will for an appreciable period of time. But I have given an account of that in another place.[1]

[1] *The Human Body* (New York: Alfred A. Knopf; 1927), page 144.

I cannot forbear, since the topic is medical, at this point, to direct attention to the medical conversations of Bob Sawyer and Ben Allen. There is one in Chapter XXX, when they are first introduced at the Dell, another in Chapter XXXII, when Mr. Pickwick and his friends attend a party at Mr. Sawyer's rooms in Lant Street. This was used by Dickens for one of his readings. And well it might be, for into that scene there drops the most astounding medical man in life or literature, Mr. Jack Hopkins. It is a thoroughly Dickensian performance; Mr. Hopkins appears just for a moment, a fleeting glimpse, but there he is, for ever in our lives. And last, the evening with Mr. Winkle in the surgery in Bristol.

They are all excellent. A weak word — they are, in fact, the best in literature. They are almost the only good ones in literature. The nearest approach to them are Conan Doyle's stories in *Round the Red Lamp* and his *Stark Munro Letters*. The superiority Dickens retained over Conan Doyle was that he caught the cynical and case-hardened humour of the young practitioner.

But here alone, in *Pickwick* and Conan Doyle, with the possible exception of Smollett's *Peregrine Pickle* (a Bath practitioner, by the way), *Roderick Random*, and McNeill Lyons's *Sixpenny Pieces*, do you catch the spirit of practice. It is hard to explain why

nobody else has ever caught that atmosphere. Lydgate in *Middlemarch* hasn't a trace of it. " A Doctor of the Old School " in Ian Maclaren's *Beside the Bonnie Brier Bush* is a very sound doctor story, but it hasn't the spirit of practice in it. *Rab and His Friends* is more a reminiscence than a piece of fiction. *Arrowsmith*, while it depicts accurately the modern research worker in some of his aspects, did not catch it either.

The fictionists are always trying to make the doctor out as nobly dedicated to the eradication of human suffering and the sacredness of human life. Only Dickens divined that patients are bores.

When I am in the countryside in England, I keep paraphrasing the words of Kipling and saying: " What can he know of England, who only London knows? " So many visitors to England leave London only to go on the Oxford–Stratford-on-Avon–Warwick tour and perhaps the other to Windsor, Stoke Pogis, and Eton. Anyone who has two weeks in England should spend at least one of them at Bath and make it his headquarters for trips in all directions.

For the Pickwickian one trip is, of course, to Bristol, although there is little left in Bristol to remind us of its place in *Pickwick*. But the Cathedral moved John Addington Symonds to say: " It gives me more pleasure to sit in Bristol Cathedral than in the Duomo at Milan."

I have referred to our trip to Berkeley on the way from Bristol to Gloucester.

Gloucester has one of the most interesting of English cathedrals. The cloister and its component parts — the scriptorium, lavatorium, etc. — are well preserved. Not far from Bath also is the beautiful cathedral city of Wells, with the moated Bishop's Palace. Then there are the ruins of Glastonbury, which will give you an idea of the destruction which was wrought by Henry VIII. The finest ruined abbey in England is Fountains Abbey; and if you sail from Southampton and have a day there, you should visit the two abbeys of Beaulieu and Netley.

If you wish to see more cathedrals, Exeter, which has the finest Norman transeptal towers in England, is not far from Bath; nor, in fact, is Salisbury. Plymouth is just beyond Exeter.

Across the Bristol Channel is Newport and the site of Tintern Abbey not far away, to which Wordsworth composed his Ode.

If you are a *Lorna Doone* fan, which I am not, the *Lorna Doone* country — Exmoor — can be visited between Exeter and Bath, to the north along the Bristol Channel.

BIRMINGHAM, TOWCESTER,
AND POINTS NORTH

On nearly the last day of Mr. Pickwick's incarceration in the Fleet, he was visited by Nathaniel Winkle and his new wife, formerly Miss Arabella Allen. Inasmuch as their marriage had been a runaway one, Mr. Pickwick was induced to visit Bristol in order to mollify Mr. Benjamin Allen, the bride's brother, and also to stop at Birmingham and persuade Mr. Winkle of the propriety of his son's action.

Returning from Bristol, having acquired both Ben Allen and Bob Sawyer for companions, they stayed at the Hop Pole Hotel, Tewkesbury, and at the Bell on Berkeley Heath, at the old Royal Hotel at Birmingham, at the Dun Cow at Dunchurch, and the Saracen's head at Towcester.

None but a specialist in *Pickwick* will want to visit all these places. To adapt a phrase that I understand was once in Baedeker, " If pressed for time, you may omit Cambridge," to the enragement of the members of that ancient university.

If one goes to Birmingham it will be for other than Pickwickian reasons, for there is nothing left of Mr. Pickwick's Birmingham.

Birmingham and Berkeley have historical associa-

tions for the physician, and if such you be, you should go there.

Berkeley I have mentioned in the section on Bath; it was the home of Edward Jenner. The little thatched shed where he is reputed to have taken cowpox matter from the hand of Sarah Nelmes and inoculated it into the arm of James Phipps is still there. The church where his father and brother were successively rector, maintains a brooding air of imminent dissolution. His simple tablet — with just the name and his dates — is in the chancel. But in the little town itself there is no stone or statue, no monument or inscription to its greatest citizen, and one of the world's greatest.

Mr. Pickwick's entrance into Birmingham forced the same impressions on him that occur to the modern visitor. " The straggling cottages by the road-side, the dingy hue of every object visible, the murky atmosphere, the paths of cinders and brick dust, the deep red glow of furnace fires in the distance, the volumes of dense smoking issuing heavily forth from high toppling chimneys, blackening and obscuring everything around; the glare of distant lights, the ponderous waggons which toiled along the road, laden with clashing rods of iron, or piled with heavy goods " — then, as now, proclaim a great working city.

Here James Watt and his partner, Matthew Boul-

ton, perfected the steam engine. Here in 1897 there was " a sudden development of cycle-manufacturing, followed in 1899 by an almost equally sudden collapse." Here today motor-cars and rubber tires are turned out with as much profusion as the public is capable of absorbing. Fort Dunlop, a suburb for rubber-goods workers, reminds us of our debt to the road guides of the genial-appearing founder. Birmingham has made England move.

For the medical man the suburban district of Edgbaston is of especial interest because here lived, and is buried, one of the most astute clinical observers who ever lived, William Withering, who introduced foxglove, or digitalis, into practice. My difficulties with languages prevented me from finding any of his memorials — no foreigner could ever remember how the Brummagems pronounce Edgbaston, but my friend Dr. Ralph Major, who is accomplished along those lines, once made his way there and assures me that the memorials exist.

Mr. Pickwick came to Birmingham when its real glory had departed. In the late eighteenth century as remarkable a group of men as ever forgathered were members of a friendly philosophical society in Birmingham. The leading spirit was Joseph Priestley, one of the first to recognize the presence of oxygen in the air and to study its properties. Withering was a

member of this group, as were Erasmus Darwin, Watt, and Boulton.

Aside from their solid scientific achievements, these men were leaders of liberal thought. Birmingham had established itself as a home for free thought. Under the Act of Uniformity non-conforming ministers were forbidden to live in a corporate town, but Birmingham, before the Reform Bill, in spite of its size, had the government of a manor. Priestley was friendly to the American Revolution and to the spirit of the French Revolution. The less advanced citizens of Birmingham, however, showed their disapproval of his views by burning his house and destroying his scientific apparatus and the notes of his experiments. He emigrated to America and died at Northumberland, Pennsylvania, in 1804.

The present-day visitor to Birmingham can hardly feel the spirit of its past unless he thinks of these men and their work.

Towcester, in contrast to Berkeley and Birmingham, has a distinct Pickwickian flavour. I must insist on your going to Towcester.

As Colonel Drage said to me, " You'll want to go to toast her." At least that is what I thought he said until I discovered " Toaster " was " Towcester."

" In Northamptonshire! " he added. " Best county in all England. Not far from my place. Run up there

THE DEN, EATANSWILL

THE POMFRET ARMS, TOWCESTER,

formerly the Saracen's Head

in an hour or so. There's another place near there you'll want to see — where one of your fellows came from, Sulgrave Manor, the home of the Washingtons."

The best way is to go to Northampton by train and there take a car to Towcester and to Sulgrave Manor. All of this can be done in one day — indeed, in one morning.

The Saracen's Head at Towcester is now called the Pomfret Arms, but the inevitable sign informs you that it was once the Saracen's Head " of Dickens fame." The young lady who drew me a mug of ale pointed out the exact spot where Mr. Pott and Mr. Slurk engaged in their quarrel.

The roads around Towcester and Northampton are vast improvements over those which bogged Mr. Pickwick down and compelled him to rest the night at the Saracen's Head.

An American party will certainly wish to take the one which leads to Sulgrave Manor, the ancestral home of the Washingtons. Sulgrave Manor is not on the beaten track of tourist travel, and you may expect to find yourself nearly alone in the house which has been so beautifully and carefully restored and furnished with objects of association interest. The caretaker is an old friend of my friend Colonel Drage, and rode behind him when the 21st Lancers charged at

Omdurman. It was the only time that I had ever heard any mention of Frank's military exploits.

W. E. Woodward in *George Washington, The Image and the Man* [1] gives us a good description:

" Sulgrave is a tiny manor of Northamptonshire. The country thereabouts reminds one of southern Connecticut. A panorama of white meandering roads, gently swelling hills and ancient farms. In a yard of mouldering graves stands a still and pensive church with a square tower. The gardens are full of English roses and glossy green ivy clings to the walls.

" At times the sky is flat and melancholy and a foggy mist is drawn among the trees like a torn grey veil.

" Even on the clearest days it is a quiet, brooding land. To one of vivid fancy the landscape seems to be holding its breath; there are secrets in its rustic silence. It is not at all like the glittering sun-and-sea splendour of Devon."

It is not necessary to describe the sights of the Manor House itself for you cannot escape them, once you are there.

[1] New York: Boni and Liveright; 1926.

THE BIBLIOGRAPHY OF
PICKWICK PAPERS

Of articles about *Pickwick*, there are hundreds —
too many to attempt to note in full. But *Pickwick* has
been the subject of at least seven books, full-sized
tomes:

PERCY FITZGERALD: *The History of Pickwick*. London: Chapman and Hall; 1891.

This is an elaborate attempt to identify all the
characters and all the places and to unravel a chronology.

As an example of the pains taken to prepare this
chronology, I append a part of it:

" 1827

" Dec. 23. Trundle's Wedding.

" 24. The Gabriel Grub Story.

" 25. Christmas Day — Introduction of
Bob Sawyer.

" 26. Return to London.

1828

Jan.   8.   ' Ten days or a fortnight after his return,' service of *subpœna* by Jack-
son.

"   9.   Visit to Perker.

"   10.   Bob Sawyer's Party (' the Invitation
was given at Dingley Dell for
Thursday Fortnight.')

Feb. 13.   Sam's Valentine.

"   14.   The Trial — *Bardell* v. *Pickwick*.

"   16.   Departure for, and arrival at Bath,
' to stay two months.'

"   17.   Ball at the Assembly Rooms.

"   20.   Mr. Pickwick moved to the Royal
Crescent."

The book suffers from an extreme and unnecessary
carelessness and haphazardness in arrangement, and
from lack of references to source material.

PERCY FITZGERALD: *Pickwickian Studies*. London:
New Century Press ; 1899.

These include " Ipswich," " Bath," " Old Rochester," " Goswell Street," " Mary Hogarth," etc.

It is astonishing that a man with such Pickwickian
erudition as Mr. Fitzgerald could have made so many
blunders as are to be found in this volume. My copy
is enlivened with the marginal notes of a meticulous

and extremely crotchety scholar. His caustic com-
ments on Fitzgerald's mistakes have been the most
informative sources I have used in this book.

PERCY FITZGERALD: *The Pickwickian Dictionary and
Cyclopedia.* London: Percy Fitzgerald and W. T.
Spencer; 1900.

This is a much more carefully compiled work than
the preceding. I have never failed to find a reference
I wanted, and can remember no inaccuracies.

J. R. HASSARD: *A Pickwickian Pilgrimage.* 1881.

I have never seen a copy.

JOSEPH GREGO: *Pictorial Pickwickiana. Charles
Dickens and his Illustrators.* 2 vols. London: Chapman and Hall; 1899.

The subtitle, " Charles Dickens and his Illustrators," is too comprehensive. The work is devoted entirely to *Pickwick.*

C. M. NEALE: *An Index to Pickwick.* London: Printed
for the author by J. Hitchcock, Streatham; 1897.

Practically a concordance.

SAMUEL W. LAMBERT: *When Mr. Pickwick Went Fish-
ing,* with eleven illustrations by Robert Seymour.
New York: Edmund Byrne Hackett, The Brick Row
Book Shop; 1924.

I have referred to this in connection with the Seymour controversy.

An Account of the Origin of Pickwick Papers, by MRS. SEYMOUR, *widow of the distinguished artist who Originated the work, with Mr. Dickens' version and her Reply thereto, showing the* Fallacy *of his statements: also letters of her husband and other distinguished men, with a* Preface *by* F. G. KOTTON. 50 copies only issued. 1901.

Mrs. Seymour's pamphlet, incorporated in this publication, was first published in 1854. I deeply regret I have never been able to examine a copy of this work.

There were a number of imitations of Pickwick, notably: *Pickwick Abroad, or the Tour in France,* by G. W. M. REYNOLDS. 1839. It is a weak and watery affair, but evidently, from the number of copies extant, enjoyed a certain popularity.

Prime Pickwicks in Parts, by JOHN C. ECKEL (New York: Edgar H. Wells and Company; 1928), is a bibliography of the first issue of *Pickwick Papers.*

I suppose the most intricate and technical bibliographic problem in English literature centres on *Pickwicks* in parts. The bibliographic problems of the First Folio are simple compared to it, however in-

volved the typographic problems of the First Folio
may be.

So, since I am arguing that a knowledge of *Pickwick* is an introduction to a knowledge of life, let us
examine the example of human frailty represented by
book-collecting.

He who desires to collect Dickens will find himself,
like Dante or John Bunyan at the beginning of their
adventures, in a thicket. He should start with a *Pickwick* and he will want a *Pickwick* in parts and really
a prime *Pickwick* in parts. Here his difficulties begin.

Pickwick Papers was issued in monthly parts —
each of about forty pages, with the well-known green
cover and some advertisements. It is unnecessary to
tell any publisher or beginning author that the success of the venture was by no means assured, so the
publishers printed only a limited number of copies of
the first issue. Just how many, only heaven knows.
The publishers afterwards said about four hundred.
But perhaps a thousand were printed from the original type. The first number did not sell very well, and
only five hundred copies of Part II were printed.
When Sam Weller appeared, in Part IV, the sales
leaped to forty thousand, and this popularity was
enhanced rather than abated as later issues appeared.
Naturally, those who began to be interested at the
later dates would want to obtain the earlier issues, and

equally naturally the publishers were willing to oblige and printed issues from later set-ups of type.

Then, after the second part was issued, Seymour, the original artist, died, and he was replaced first by R. W. Buss, whose illustrations for the third part were unsatisfactory, so that he was discharged, and then by Hablot Browne (" Phiz "), who was associated with Dickens for many years.

Later " Phiz " engraved a second, duplicate set of plates and also facsimiled the Seymour plates for the first collected edition. At that far time, when no one realized how valuable prime *Pickwicks* in parts were to be, plates were interchanged, facts were substituted, and all manner of outrages performed.

The result has been a turmoil which has absorbed Lilliputian scholarship to a point of frenzy.

There are those who would like to possess a complete set of *Pickwick* in parts with every part in the state of first issue. And it isn't always possible to say exactly what was the state of the first issue of everything.

Should, for instance, the Irishman's stick have a bundle on it in the first illustration in Part XVIII? All the research in Christendom has not settled that little point. In some plates the Irishman has a bundle; in some he doesn't. Some collectors, such as the late George Barr McCutcheon, have solved the matter by

buying two examples of Part XVIII. But that is obviously a mere subterfuge. It does not settle the great fundamental question, which is the first issue? It is a mere piece of arrogance. No, give me the man who comes out in the open where you can shoot at him and says: " The Irishman without the bundle is the first issue."

Imagine the discomfiture of a collector who thought he had a prime *Pickwick* in parts and then found that in the very first plate Mr. Pickwick's buttons were on the left side of his vest. Would not the whole world turn to dust and ashes in his mouth?

The famous eleven points that make a prime *Pickwick* in parts are as follows, according to Mr. Eckel:

1. All covers of the parts must bear the date 1836 in Roman numbers.

2. Parts I and II must have the words: " With four illustrations by Seymour."

3. Part III, the words " With illustrations by R. W. Buss."

4. Part I must have three plates by Seymour, signed, and not re-etched by " Phiz."

5. Part II must have three plates by Seymour signed.

6. Part III must have two plates signed " Drawn and etched by R. W. Buss," and the pages numbered thereon.

7. Part IV, two plates faintly signed " Nemo " and not " Phiz."

8. Parts II, III, X, and XV must have the addresses by the Author.

9. Parts XVII, XVIII, and XX the addresses by the publishers.

10. Plates in Parts I to XII must have no captions, only numerical references to the pages where they go, parts XIII to XX have neither titles nor numerical references.

11. On the vignette title-page the name " Weller " on the signboard over the door is spelled with a " V." On the frontispiece the artist's name on the center shield on the bottom must run around the shield.

Some of the things that can be wrong in the illustrations are as follows:

" Part I

" (a) Pickwick's buttons should be on the right side of the vest. Signed faintly by Seymour on the lower left. Page 2, with a slight curl to the ' g ' in ' page.' . . .

" (c) The trigger *must* be on the gun. Signed by Seymour in lower center. Page 9.

Part IV

" Two plates by Hablot K. Browne. The first plate (The Breakdown) is faintly signed ' Nemo ' on lower

left. Page 89. The second plate which introduced Sam
Weller is signed ' Nemo ' on lower right. Page 94.
Second state of these plates shows additional detail
work.

Part VI

" The bird cage rests on the boughs of the tree.
Signed ' Phiz del.' Page 169.

" The bell hangs to the right of the door. Signed
' Phiz del.' Page 154.

Part VII

" There are two donkeys in the Pound with Mr.
Pickwick. Signed ' Phiz del.' Page 197.

" Sam Weller's legs are together in Dodson &
Fogg's Office. Signed ' Phiz del.' Page 201.

Part X

" The cat and dog must be in the foreground.
Signed ' Phiz del.' Page 296. In the Gabriel Grub
plate there should be a face in the tree ; the bone must
be far away from the skull, and there is no tombstone
in the lower right corner. Signed ' Phiz del.' Page 301.

Part XI

" ' Mr. Pickwick slides.' There are four stumps in
the foreground on the ice. Arabella's left foot is forward. There are no flying birds. Church spire very
faint in the background. The dog is black. Signed
' Phiz del.' Page 313.

Part XII

" There is no hat on the front bench in the Trial scene. Signed ' Phiz del.' Page 358.

Part XV

" There is no loop at the end of the clothes-line; the loop is present in the second state.

Part XVI

" Sam Weller's hat must have the cockade. There must be a railing on the left of the steps. Both these details were omitted when re-drawn.

Parts XIX–XX

" The knife in the hand of the Fat Boy points downward; a saltcellar rests on the table."

There are very few pundits who have ever acquired full authority on the points of *Pickwick*. Their persons are naturally guarded with extreme care by their respective governments because the Herculean training required to achieve this body of knowledge should not be wasted.

There are said to be fourteen or fifteen prime *Pickwicks* in existence. Aside from their intrinsic interest as literature, they have a certain material value, as may be indicated from the following:

" The record price of $16,300 paid by Mr. Cole on

December 7, 1927, for the Hatton copy, presents some interesting twists on figures. The original parts cost 25 cents each when issued or $5.00 for all the units. At the price mentioned, the copy brought 3,260 times the original value. Each part sold for $801.50. In the book there were 609 pages to which is to be added 16 pages of preliminary matter, thus making a total of 625 pages. Therefore each page fetched $26.33."

" Beginning with the earliest-known auction records of *Pickwicks*, it is interesting to note the marvellous stride in prices. Comparison of their records show the last copy sold brought more than thirty times as much as the first which was sold at Sotheby's in 1896, thirty-two years ago."

For the collector, the most treasured copy is the one presented to Mary Hogarth with Dickens's signature. It is owned by Mr. Elkins of Philadelphia. When Harry B. Smith purchased it for William Wright he paid about $500. Its present value is conjectural, but it must be about $25,000.

In 1908 a prime copy in America brought $1,450 as a purchase price.

In 1916 the Coggeshall copy brought $5,350. Later it was sold for $11,000.

In 1925 the Bruton copy was sold for $5,500. A few years later it brought $8,000.

The George Barr McCutcheon copies sold for about $7,000 and $5,750.

What will be the next price?

The expenditure of all this wealth for a few pamphlets bound in green and containing a prose narrative which can be purchased elsewhere verbatim for less than one dollar must give social philosophers the shudders. What plans are the soviet governments of the future going to make for these " collectors," who fulfil no useful function and upset the economic standards? For they will make a place for themselves, you know, just like termites.

I have no doubt, in fact, that Stalin preserves and cherishes some such thing as a first edition of the pamphlet containing Lenin's first address to the Soviet Congress, although his cold logical mind would assure him that he could obtain a later reprint which would do just as well; no, an aura hangs around the original.

In the meantime, since I am not in the 16,000-dollar-a-book class, I will prefer my Topical Edition of *Pickwick*, edited by C. van Noorden, a remarkable instance of devotion to a book. Mr. van Noorden has collected photographs or pictures of every place, article of furniture or of commerce (such as a picture of the " common profeel machine," alluded to by Sam Weller, or a " Pope Joan board "), has run down

every contemporary allusion, reference, or analogy in the book. The result is the supreme edition of *Pick-wick*. If my copy could not be replaced, I would not exchange it for the finest prime parts extant.

Only second is the Jubilee Edition, which did in part what Mr. van Noorden did so completely.

Then, if you really crave a *Pickwick* in parts, there is the Lombard Street Edition, in which each part has been reproduced as issued; and they look and read like the originals. For all practical purposes they are as good as the originals. And I can feel the shiver of horror that runs through the Grolier Club as I pen these lines.

SUMMARY

of Places Mentioned in PICKWICK PAPERS
or Associated with it

LONDON

Goswell Street — Where Mr. Pickwick lived, now Goswell Road.

Lant Street — in which were Bob Sawyer's lodgings, in Southwark, over London Bridge on the south bank of the Thames.

Guildhall — In the Court of Common Pleas, here, the trial of Bardell v. Pickwick was heard. The Guildhall is a familiar " sight " of London. The home of Gog and Magog. Behind Saint Paul's.

Dulwich — Scene of Mr. Pickwick's retirement. Suburb of London.

Brick Lane — Off Hanbury Street, which is off Commercial Street. Commercial Street continues from Aldgate (behind the Bank). At 160 the Brick Lane Branch of the United Grand Ebenezer Temperance Association met.

Dickens House — 48 Doughty Street. Where

Pickwick Papers was finished. Now a Dickens memorial and museum.

Holborn and Furnival Street — The Prudential Insurance Company Building. Site of Furnival's Inn, where *Pickwick Papers* was begun.

South Kensington Museum — See the largest collection of original Dickens manuscripts here.

Montague Place — Off Russell Square, just behind the British Museum. Home of Mr. Perker.

Spaniards Inn — Hampstead. Scene of the apprehension of Mrs. Bardell. (Visit Keats's house and Kenwood on the same trip.)

Inns of Court — Gray's Inn, Clifford's Inn (from Fleet Street), etc. Mentioned in Chapter XXI.

BATH

The scene of many adventures of the Pickwickians — the Footmen's Swarry; Mr. Winkle's unfortunate experience with Mrs. Dowler and the sedan-chair.

The old city is fully described in *Pickwick*. The visitor must see the bronze plaque on the wall of the Grand Pump Room Hotel; the Abbey, the Assembly Rooms; the Baths; the Crescent; the Circus; Queen's Square; the Museum.

By rail Bath is reached in about 2½ hours from London, on the London, Midland and Scottish Railway from Euston Station.

BERKELEY

At the Bell at Berkeley Heath the Pickwickians lunched on the way to Birmingham. North of Bristol near the Severn. At Berkeley itself Edward Jenner performed the first vaccination against smallpox.

While in the neighbourhood be sure to visit Gloucester.

BIRMINGHAM

Where in Chapter XLIX Mr. Pickwick's interview with Mr. Winkle senior is recounted. The Old Royal Hotel, which is the only Birmingham landmark mentioned in *Pickwick*, has been torn down.

BRISTOL

Comes into the story twice. First the Bush Inn, Bristol, is Mr. Winkle's refuge when he flees the wrath of Dowler. In Bristol Mr. Bob Sawyer and Mr. Ben Allen have set up medical practice.

Can be easiest visited by bus from Bath. No Pickwickian landmarks remain, but the Cathedral and the Cabot Tower excite interest.

BURY ST. EDMUNDS

Scene of Mr. Pickwick's adventure at the girls' school. Also his attack of rheumatism, necessitating his being trundled in a wheelbarrow,

and his incarceration in the pound by Captain
Boldwig.

Bury St. Edmunds is in Suffolk, some ninety miles
northeast of London. It can be reached by the
London and North-Eastern Railway from Liverpool Street Station.

COBHAM

in Kent, five miles from Rochester. At the Leather
Bottle Inn Mr. Tupman retired after his hu-
miliation by Mr. Jingle and the maiden aunt. A
pleasant walk from Rochester.

COVENTRY

One of the stages where Messrs. Pickwick, Allen,
and Sawyer stopped on the way from Birmingham to London. Chapter LI.

DAVENTRY AND DUNCHURCH

See Coventry.

DORKING

Where Mrs. Weller senior kept the Marquis of
Granby. Two inns are to be seen there today —
the King's Arms and the King's Head. Dorking
is a small market town southwest of London, between Guildford and Reigate.

IPSWICH

At the White Horse Hotel Mr. Pickwick had the
adventure with the lady in the yellow curl-

papers. At the home of Mr. Nupkins, Mr. Pickwick encountered Jingle, and Sam Weller met the pretty housemaid. Chapters XXII to XXV, inclusive.

Ipswich is in Suffolk about a hundred miles from London on the line of the London, North-Eastern Railway, reached from Liverpool Street Station.

NORWICH

The Pickwickians took the Norwich coach in order to reach Eatanswill. Whether Norwich is actually Eatanswill is debatable. It is situated in Norfolk about 165 miles northeast of London, and is reached by the London and North-Eastern Railway from Liverpool Street Station.

The home of Sir Thomas Browne and George Borrow, it has a gem of a Cathedral and many other interesting antiquities.

ROCHESTER

The first objective of the Pickwickians' pilgrimage. The Bull Hotel, where they stayed, is still " intact." The Theatre Royal, the Castle, the Cathedral, all mentioned, are objects of interest to visitors. Rochester figures in the last of Dickens's novels — the unfinished *Mystery of Edwin Drood* — under the name of Cloisterham.

Visit, near by, Cobham, Cobtree, Sandling, and
Gad's Hill, Dickens's last home.

SUDBURY

Usually identified as Eatanswill. Not far from
Ipswich.

TEWKSBURY

Here Mr. Pickwick and his companions stopped for
dinner on the way to Birmingham — at the Hop
Pole, which is still " intact."

TOWCESTER

On the way from Birmingham to London the rain
caused Mr. Pickwick to stay overnight at the
Saracen's Head here. The Saracen's Head is now
called the Pomfret Arms, but a notice near the
coaching entrance identifies it with the old Saracen's Head. The room in which the encounter
between Mr. Pott and Mr. Slurk took place is
on view. Towcester is near Northampton and
can best be reached by motor from there. While
there, plan to have your visit include Sulgrave
Manor, the ancestral home of the Washingtons.

Fictional Places Mentioned

DINGELY DELL

The home of the Wardles. It is somewhere in the
neighbourhood of Rochester, certainly — probably Cobtree, Sandling, is meant.

EATANSWILL

May be Norwich, or, more likely, Sudbury, which is on the lower border of Suffolk, about eighty miles northeast of London. The Rose and Crown has been identified with the Town Arms.

MUGGLETON

The Muggleton cricket team played Dingley Dell. Probably Maidstone was meant, as the prototype of Muggleton.

A NOTE ON THE TYPE IN
WHICH THIS BOOK IS SET

*This book is composed (on the lino-
type), in Scotch. There is a diver-
gence of opinion regarding the exact
origin of this face, some authorities
holding that it was first cut by
Alexander Wilson & Son, of Glasgow, in 1837; others trace it back
to a modernized Caslon old style
brought out by Mrs. Henry Caslon
in 1796 to meet the demand for modern faces resulting from the popularity of the Bodoni types. Whatever
its origin, it is certain that the face
was widely used in Scotland, where
it was called Modern Roman, and
since its introduction into America it
has been known as Scotch. The es-
sential characteristics of the Scotch
face are its sturdy capitals, its full
rounded lower case, the graceful
fillet of its serifs, and the general
effect of crispness*

COMPOSED, PRINTED, AND BOUND BY
THE PLIMPTON PRESS, NORWOOD, MASS.
PAPER MADE BY CURTIS & BROTHER,
NEWARK, DEL.